GROUNDWORK

GroundWork

New and Selected Poems of Don L. Lee/Haki R. Madhubuti from 1966-1996

Haki R. Madhubuti

With a Foreword by Gwendolyn Brooks
and
Preface by Bakari Kitwana

Third World Press
Chicago

Third World Press, Chicago 60619

Printed in the United States of America

05 04 03 02 01 00 99 98 97 96   5 4 3 2 1

ISBN: 0-88378-172-7 (hardcover)
       0-88378-173-5 (paperback)

Library of Congress Cataloging-in-Publication Data

Madhubuti, Haki R., 1942-
       GroundWork: New and Selected Poems of Don L.
    Lee/Haki R. Madhubuti from 1966-1996 / with foreword
    by Gwendolyn Brooks and preface by Bakari Kitwana.
    — 1st ed.
       p.   cm.
    Includes bibliographical references.
       1. Afro-American men—Poetry.
       2. Afro-Americans—Poetry.
    I. Title. II. Title: GroundWork
    PS3563.A3397A6   1997
    811'.54—DC20
                                              96-30118
                                                  CIP

DEDICATION

To
Vivian V. Gordon
Toni Cade Bambara
Arthur P. Davis
Henry Blakely II
Oscar Brown III
Naikwa Jawole Nini Tasleem Nurullah

To the children of Liberia, Rwanda, Burundi, and Bosnia

for the poets of the Black Arts who live their lives
for their art and their people
and understand quite eloquently
the essential quality and necessity of both
and have made a great sacrifice,
a deep and a special commitment
that is required in the United States
to serve their people and be heard on their own terms.

Gwendolyn Brooks   Dudley Randall   Amiri Baraka   Mari Evans

Sonia Sanchez   Kalamu ya Salaam   Lucille Clifton

and

for my children

CONTENTS

8 *KILLING MEMORY, SEEKING ANCESTORS* (1987)

FOREWORD

Haki: artist, pioneer, "loyalist." Haki developed a *communicating* expression that suited his direct and earnest concepts. More than any other Black poet who became influential in the late Sixties, he remained actively loyal to the richness of his faith in and love for Black people. He scolds them now and then, but only as a benevolent father would scold them—aching in his awareness of how much there is to hurt them, in themselves and outside themselves—aching in his wish that they maintain integrity and a decent Family loyalty. He has influenced many Black poets, Hispanic poets, and, strangely, Caucasian poets who sensed a vibrant vigor in his dealings with language, and admired it, respected it.

Haki has said:

> "What writers write tells to what extent they are involved with the real world....Writers should be questioners of the world and doers within the world. Question everything. And don't be satisfied with the quick surface answers....Bad writing containing the most 'revolutionary' idea is, first and last, bad writing. A high standard must be met if the writer is to communicate effectively. The ability to develop a style that is clear, original, and communicative is what separates writers from non-writers."

Many years ago I said of his style and commitment (interchangeable) what is mercilessly true today:

> He knows that nothing human is elegant. He is not interested in modes of writing that aspire to elegance. He is well-acquainted with "elegant" literature (what hasn't he read?) but, while certainly respecting the advantages and influence of good workmanship, he is not interested in supplying the needs of the English Departments at Harvard and Oxford nor the editors of Partisan Review, although he could serve, mightily, as fact factory for these. He speaks to Blacks hungry for what they themselves refer to as

"real poetry." These Blacks find themselves and the stuff of their existence in his healthy, lithe, lusty reaches of free verse. The "last thing" these people crave is elegance. It is very hard to enchant, with elegant song, the ears of a fellow whose stomach is growling. You can't be heard. The more interesting noise is too loud.

And of course Haki was always interested in reaching "those people."

Haki, at times, has been called a "racist."

I define racism as prejudice *with* oppression. That is: you are permitted to detest green eyes. That's all right. That's *personal*. What you are *not* permitted to do is kill every green-eyed individual you encounter. That's *not* all right. That's OPPRESSION.

Haki is not a killer. He is a lover of humanity, of what is human. He is an interpreter and a protector of Blackness. He is a subscriber to what is beautiful in the world.

Long ago Haki defined Black poetry. He considered it a working beauty fully able to nourish and extend Black people. (*That* is the ultimate meaning of his essential definition.)

In this foreword I am *not* assaulting our mutual understanding that there are respectable Black uniquities. However, today many Black poets are flopping off in worrisome directions. Many of them do not know *what* to do or be. Many of them want above *all* things *not* to be Black. Black people who want above all things not to be Black are the most pitiable *and* comical people in the world. The poets among such *fight* Blackness with every punch and pout in their power. Such people are very busy imitating some of the new moderns, manufacturers of chopped-up journalism, dazed and dopey. Such people have been fondled and adopted by non-spunky white poets and critics who of course have *no* interest in preserving, in *enfirming* the bolts, the binders of Blackness. They would *like* Blackness to disappear altogether.

Said and says Haki: "The Black writer learns from the people....Black artists are culture stabilizers, bringing back old values, and introducing new ones."

I long ago decided he is a further pioneer and a positive prophet, a prophet not afraid to be positive even *though* aware of a daily evolving, of his own sober and firm churning. He is a toughness. He is not a superficial toughness. He is the kind of toughness that doesn't just "sass its mammy" but goes right through to the bone.

GWENDOLYN BROOKS

PREFACE

"This is a historic moment," Haki began in the prophetic, contemplative tone that has become his trademark. Backstage at Harlem's legendary Apollo Theater in a cramped 10-foot square room that had easily tripled its comfort capacity, Madhubuti's poetic words, like the solemn eyes that brightened the room, defined the sacred hour. Harlem, Black America's cultural mecca, is not an easy place to make history. But in the tiny well-lit room, shoulder to shoulder, with William Kunstler, Percy Sutton, Louis Farrakhan, Betty Shabazz, Congressman Charles Rangel and others, none denied the night's significance. Moments later, Betty Shabazz and Louis Farrakhan brought closure to years of division between the Shabazz and Farrakhan families.

Few knew that Haki Madhubuti was instrumental in bringing the two together. An unusual place for a poet? Haki Madhubuti is not your usual poet. He has centered much of his life in such moments of quiet reflection, pondering the significance of Black world culture and politics. He is an early riser. "I like to rise with the sun," he often says of his body clock which has him in motion by 5 a.m. on most days. He is a quick-study, and slices meticulously through what he considers must-reading with a routine that most apply to their favorite TV sitcoms. "Reading must become like eating...done daily and consuming the best," he advises.

Much of this study, when combined with life experience and poetic meditation, is evident in the depth and range of these long overdue collected poems, *GroundWork*. *GroundWork* finally brings together in one volume some of the best of Madhubuti's poetry, demonstrating his progression across four critical decades. However, *GroundWork* is more than a book of Black poetry's signifyin,' rhymes, and rhythms. It is a painfully honest critique of the transformative late 1960s, the integrated 1970s, the African-centered 1980s, and the turbulent early 1990s. Beyond the historical journey, the poems revel in the timelessness and multiplicity of Blackness: Black language, Black love, Black dignity, Black strength, Black weakness, and

Black possibility. Earlier poems like "But he was Cool," "One Sided Shoot-out," "Big Momma," and "The Secrets of the Victor" rekindle images of the fiery Don L. Lee of the Black Arts Movement. We see some of these dimensions at work in this excerpt from "A Poem to Compliment Other Poems:"

> change nigger change.
> know the realenemy.
> change: is us is or is u aint. change. now now
>   read a change. live a change. read a
>   blackpoem.
>   change. be the realpeople.
>   change. black poems
> will change:
> know the realenemy. change. know the realenemy.
>   change yr/enemy. change. know the real
> change know the realenemy change, change,
>   change

More recent poems like "Haiti," "B-Network," "Mothers," "Rwanda," and "White People are People Too" reveal that the former Lee turned Madhubuti has made a graceful transition. Now a seasoned poet with Black fire and militancy still in his soul, Madhubuti blends prose with poetry and is even more determined to revive Blackness in us. Consider the poem "Killing Memory:"

> people
> of colors and voices
> are locked in multibasement state buildings
> stealing memories
> more efficient
> than vultures tearing flesh
> from
> decaying bodies.
>
> the order is that the people are to
> believe and believe
> questioning or contemplating

the direction of the weather is
unpatriotic.

it is not that we distrust poets and politicians.

we fear the disintegration of thought,
we fear the cheapening of language,
we fear the history of victims and the loss of vision,
we fear writers whose answer to
maggots drinking from the open
wounds of babies
is
to cry genocide while demanding
ten cents per word and
university chairs.
we fear politicians
that sell coffins at a discount
and consider ideas blasphemy
as young people world over bleed from the teeth
    while
aligning themselves with whoever
brings the food.
whoever brings the love.

who speaks the language of
bright memory?

who speaks the language of
necessary memory?

The impact of Haki Madhubuti is found in his crisp, clear understanding of white world supremacy as it has and continues to impact Blacks around the globe. This is his undying contribution to Black struggle. This is his mission. Make no mistake; there is no ethnic cheerleading here. His is a commitment to Blackness that is unapologetic, well-studied, consistent, and not built on anti-whiteness. Neither is this opportunism. His is a sincere love for Black people. Along with other activist-intellectuals, Madhubuti has been at the forefront of constructing a practical African-centered worldview that is rooted in Black world history, struggle, culture, spirituality and contemporary reality. Madhubuti's ideas are not built on disjointed pseudo science nor far fetched delusions. Neither is he a strict, bookish intellectual, bogged down in the rhetoric of the academy. In 1983, historian Lerone Bennett, Jr. described Madhubuti as " a spokesman for a new poetry and a new Black vision." Bennett continued, "As a poet, theoretician and organizer, he played a pivotal role in raising the level of consciousness of millions of Blacks."

Feel his politics and his passion in the titles he chooses for his books. Think Black. Black Pride. Don't Cry, Scream. We Walk the Way of the New World. Book of Life. From Plan to Planet: The Need for Afrikan Minds and Institutions. Enemies: The Clash of Races. Earthquakes and Sunrise Missions. Killing Memory, Seeking Ancestors. Black Men: Obsolete, Single, Dangerous?; The Afrikan American Family in Transition. Claiming Earth: Race, Rage, Rape, Redemption; Blacks Seeking a Culture of Enlightened Empowerment. A cursory reading of his poems and essays makes clear that his political thought reaches far beyond critics' charge of "narrow nationalism" or "protest writer." He has tested theory in the practical world of building institutions because, as he puts it, "that's what our best minds and political theorists have led us to understand is our salvation. America is not going to change. White supremacy is a growth industry. Our future is in independent Black institutions."

In the late 1960s, Madhubuti was involved in the Congress of Racial Equality (CORE), the Student Non-Violent Coordinating Committee (SNCC), the Southern Christian Leadership Conference (SCLC) and the Organization of Black American Culture (OBAC). The Congress of Afrikan People in the 1970s, the National Black United Front in the 1980s, and in the 1990s the National Black Wholistic Society and the Million Man March Executive Committee have all felt his influence. His efforts, along with countless other Chicago activists, in building the Institute of Positive Education, Third World Press, and the New Concept School—a 26 year-old independent Black school for children—are legendary.

Clearly, his poetry is political and his politics are the essence of his poetry. One of the primary poets of the Black Arts Movement, Madhubuti has long recognized the intimate relationship between art and reality. In his life and work are countless lessons for today's new Black poets, hip-hop artists. Many are in search of empowering language. Many realize that their role is to keep the Black vernacular alive in public space. In his 60s and 70s poetry, Madhubuti similarly brought the language of everyday Black people to the public arena, stretching and chopping language in the Black oral tradition. Many hip-hop artists are in search of independence and control as artists. Many are concerned about Blacks' limited influence over the art and culture they create. Madhubuti's career as poet and publisher is instructive. His home has always been the independent Black press. From his early days with Dudley Randall's Broadside Press to the creation of Third World Press, Madhubuti ritualized the message in his work. "It made no sense to me to talk bad about white folks and then beg them to publish it."

His personal journey from a poverty-stricken Detroit childhood to author, publisher, and educator is no American dream of tragedy and triumph. He does not find refuge in bootstrap Americanisms. American reality, not dream, again and again returns him to scorched earth. His understanding of the power of multinational corporate structures and their influence in strengthening white world supremacy played a large role in his independent development. Thus, in an age of downsizing and cutbacks, neither his work, nor his ideas have become casualties of corporate culture.

In 1969 David Llorens said of Madhubuti, "It is not enough that we might consciously identify with the sentiments finding expression in his words. There is a subconscious, where words do not reach but voice is not to be denied. And the voice of Don Lee is faithful to its master, resonant, haunting, leaving in the distance all manner of half-truths. Transcending customs. Niceties. Platitudes. Seeking no approval. No applause. No contest. Just making people hear their own silence. A disquieting experience." Over the years, Madhubuti—as poet, activist, institution-builder, and intellectual—has stayed true to this mission. This is the gift of this volume.

In the introduction to his widely acclaimed *Black Men: Obsolete, Single, Dangerous?*, Madhubuti wrote, "I consider myself primarily a poet. I'm a poet in the Afrikan griot tradition, a keeper of the culture's history, short and tall tales, a rememberer." As a cultural rememberer, as one who understands the power of the word, Madhubuti demonstrates that this ground work has been his life calling. Who will speak the day-to-day triumphs and failures of a people, offering hope and vision, if not its poets? Amidst the cacophony of Black-faced spokespersons who celebrate Black heterogeneity, who will paint a clear, concise and an uncensored picture of the survival and development of a whole people? Here, at the dawn of the 21st century, in the throes of a new global economy, it is a good time to revisit these four important decades in preparation for what lies ahead. *GroundWork* is a ready medium.

BAKARI KITWANA

INTRODUCTION

These poems cover a thirty-year period (1966-1996) in which I was involved in profound and intense political and personal struggle. They represent a life, my life. They represent my political, cultural, and personal transitions. They represent early life and my passage to middle age. Herein are youthful naiveté and idealism; a deep commitment to my people and others; and a search for a belief system (spiritual and political) that was/is not oppressive, dogmatic, incorrect, self-righteous, or demeaning, but one that is wholesome and wholistic, progressive and fair, spiritually inclusive, artistically stimulating, and children-centered.

This is a life's work and therefore is a life's dedication to an artform and to a people's authentic, cultural survival and development. This must not be minimized. I believe in the power of art, that it is essential for the empowerment of any people's cultural expression. I do not think that one artform (poetry) is enough to guarantee the cultural substance of a person or a people. We are too complex and too influenced by mass media, mass religions, and a secular world that fights each other hourly for our souls.

A great many of our souls, or as others may prefer our minds, are indeed ripe for conversion. However, as a poet of African ancestry and Black cultural movements, I do not claim, nor want my work to be *the* answer to the fundamental questions nagging at the consciousness of most thinking Black folks/Africans in America: Who am I?, What is my role in the world?, How shall I and my loved ones practice our indigenous culture and worship the God(s) of our foreparents/people without excuse, shame, or apology? and Why are we poor and what path(s) lead to our empowerment? Answering these questions takes serious study and committed action, and fundamental to such actions is conflict. This conflict is not necessarily due to the nature or content of the questions and the acts themselves, but because such questions require practices which take place in Western culture that is often hostile and has already laid claim to its own authenticity. This culture views most things (acts) outside of its definition and province as strange, anti-American, anti-Christian, anti-white, and therefore suspect and deserving of investigation, whitelisting, discredit, neutralization, and ridicule.

Poetry has informed my life. It has given to me the one quality that has served me and my work to this day, the quality of doubt, a healthy skepticism. Also there is an understanding that life and art are diverse, difficult, and intricate and that neither is possible without the other. There can not be art without life nor life without art. Neither can be fully lived or understood by seeking and accepting easy answers. Yes, education is part of the answer, but all too often the debate is reduced to whose education? Poetry in concert with the other artforms (music, dance, visual art, drama, fiction, film, literary non-fiction, and my respect for and practice of spiritual enlightenment) is at the core of what energizes and empowers me. Poetry has forced me to question most things and to go subsurface for the solutions.

The work here, in all of its bone-bracing energy, is the result of a life lived as a poet-activist, political person, freedom fighter, businessman, family man, and institution builder. This work should be read and understood in a historical and cultural context. This is how it was created and how it should be received. I did not, nor do I now write in an apolitical or ahistorical vacuum. My environment is critical and essential to my understanding of the world and my (our) place in it. Growing up poor automatically positioned me with the overwhelming majority of the world's people and I didn't need Marx to tell me to fight oppression, whether economic or political.

Poetry has indeed informed and textured my life. Without the work of Langston Hughes, Gwendolyn Brooks, Dudley Randall, Amiri Baraka, Margaret Walker Alexander, Margaret Danner, Melvin Tolson, Jean Toomer, Claude McKay, Sterling Brown, Robert Hayden, Mari Evans, Sonia Sanchez, Etheridge Knight, Lucille Clifton, Larry Neal, Carolyn Rodgers, Sterling Plumpp, Johari Amini, Pearl Cleage, Ishmael Reed, Useni Eugene Perkins, Naomi Long Madgett, Norman Jordan, Alice Walker, Murry DePillers, Calvin Jones, Tom Feelings, Kalamu ya Salaam, and countless other Black and non-Black poets, my work would not exist. I do not wish to minimize the influence of Black music or the other artforms, but it is the poetry and the poets who have especially given me strength and encouragement. The work of Richard Wright, W.E.B. DuBois, James Baldwin, Hoyt W. Fuller, Malcolm X, Chancellor Williams, John Henrik Clarke, Frantz Fanon, Harold Cruse, Maulana Karenga, Soyini Walton, Barbara Sizemore, Dolores E. Cross, Wesley Snipes, Walter Mosley, Toni Morrison, Ayi Kwei Armah, and Margaret Burroughs have also been essential.

From my birth in Little Rock, Arkansas in 1942, to my young years in the streets of Detroit and Chicago, to my three years in the United States Army, to my early involvement in the civil rights and Black empowerment movements of the '60s, to my struggles in the African liberation movements of the '70s, to my travels to the African, European, and Asian worlds, to my deep study of the defining texts of many cultures, to my devotion to my family, extended family, and people, I have modestly and somewhat exhaustively been a witness to the possibilities of good life, spiritual and cultural awakening, harmony, and peace in this world. As you read these poems try to visualize the growth of a *negro* boy into a *Black* young man fighting for meaning and empowerment as a mature man of *African* ancestry in white *America*.

Though not an autobiography, *GroundWork* is a cultural journey through poetry. This journey is still unfolding and has not been easy. However, I would not trade my life with anyone and therefore in this collection I am saying, *Yes*. Yes to my(our) struggles, disappointments, mistakes, accomplishments, questions, imperfections, possibilities, and victories. Finally, in a world often hostile and most certainly not of my creation, I've made and will continue to make a contribution. *GroundWork* represents a significant portion of my humble, yet incomplete journey.

H.R.M.
May 1996

Note:

In my earlier works I spell Africa with a "k" rather than a "c" because for many activists the "k" represented an acknowledgement that Africa is not the true name of our continent. The Afrika spelled with a "k" represented a redefined and potentially different Africa, and, for me, symbolized a coming back together of African people worldwide. Let it be understood that when I speak of Africa/Afrika and when most whites think of Africa, we are coming from two different worldviews. Nonetheless, in my works written after the abolishment of apartheid in South Africa, I use the 'c' spelling in order to celebrate this significant change.

In my later works I use a capital "B" when referring to Black people. The word "Black" is descriptive, but also it is a political and cultural term that identifies people of African descent at a world level.

GROUNDWORK

1
THINK BLACK!
(1966)

INTRODUCTION TO THINK BLACK!

I was born into slavery in Feb. of 1942. In the spring of that same year 110,000 persons of Japanese descent were placed in protective custody by the white people of the United States. Two out of every three of these were American citizens by birth; the other third were aliens forbidden by law to be citizens. No charges had been filed against these people nor had any hearing been held. The removal of these people was on racial or ancestral grounds only. World War II, the war against racism; yet no Germans or other enemy aliens were placed in protective custody. There should have been Japanese writers directing their writings toward Japanese audiences.

Black. Poet. Black poet am I. This should leave little doubt in the minds of anyone as to which is first. Black art is created from black forces that live within the body. Direct and meaningful contact with Black people will act as energizers for the Black forces. Black art will elevate and enlighten our people and lead them toward an awareness of self, i.e., their Blackness. It will show them mirrors. Beautiful symbols. And will aid in the destruction of anything nasty and detrimental to our advancement as a people. Black art is a reciprocal art. The Black writer learns from his people and because of his insight and "know how" he is able to give back his knowledge to the people in a manner in which they can identify, learn, and gain some type of mental satisfaction, e.g., rage or happiness. We must destroy Faulkner, dick, jane, and other perpetuators of evil. It's time for Du Bois, Nat Turner and Kwame Nkrumah. As Frantz Fanon points out: destroy the culture and you destroy the people. This must not happen. Black artists are culture stabilizers; bringing back old values, and introducing new ones. Black art will talk to the people and with the will of the people, stop the impending "protective custody."

America calling.
negroes.
can you dance?
play foot/baseball?

5

nanny?
cook?
needed now. negroes
who can entertain
ONLY.
others not
wanted.
(& are considered extremely dangerous.)

d.l.l.

BACK AGAIN, HOME

(confessions of an ex-executive)

Pains of insecurity surround me;
    shined shoes,
    conservative suits,
    button down shirts with silk ties.
    bi-weekly payroll.

Ostracized, but not knowing why;
    executive haircut,
    clean shaved,
    "yes" instead of "yeah" and "no" instead of "naw,"
    hours, nine to five. (after five he's alone)

"Doing an excellent job, keep it up;"
    promotion made—semimonthly payroll,
    very quiet—never talks,
    budget balanced—saved the company money,
    quality work—production tops.
    He looks sick. (but there is a smile in his eyes)

He resigned, we wonder why;
    let his hair grow—a mustache too,
    out of a job—broke and hungry,
    friends are coming back—bring food,
    not quiet now—trying to speak,
    what did he say?

    "Back Again,

        BLACK AGAIN,

           Home."

"STEREO"

I can clear a beach or swimming pool without
      touching water.

I can make a lunch counter become deserted
      in less than an hour.

I can make property value drop by being seen
      in a realtor's tower.

I ALONE can make the word of God have little
      or no meaning to many
      in Sunday morning's prayer hour.

I have Power,

BLACK POWER.

8

WAKE-UP NIGGERS

(you ain't part Indian)

were
don eagle & gorgeous george
sisters
or did they just
    act that way—
in the ring,
in alleys,
in bedrooms of the future.
      (continuing to take yr / money)
have you ever
heard tonto say:
    "I'm part negro?"
    (in yr / moma's dreams)
the only time
tonto was hip
was when he said:
    "what you mean WE,
    gettum up scout"
& left
that mask man
burning on a stake
    crying for satchal page
to throw his
balls
back.

&
you followed him niggers—
all of you—
    yes you did,
      I saw ya.
on yr/tip toes
with
roller skates
on yr/knees
    following Him

down the road,
                    not up
following Him
that whi
te man with
that
cross on his back.

RE-ACT FOR ACTION

(for brother H. Rap Brown)

re-act to animals:
cage them in zoos.
re-act to inhumanism:
make them human.
re-act to nigger toms:
with spiritual acts of love & forgiveness
or with real acts of force.
re-act to yr/self:
or are u too busy tryen to be cool
like tony curtis & twiggy?
re-act to whi-te actors:
understand their actions;
faggot actions & actions against
yr/dreams.
re-act to yr/brothers & sisters:
love.
re-act to whi-te actions:
with real acts of blk/action.
BAM BAM BAM

re-act to act against actors
who act out pig-actions against
your acts & actions that keep
you re-acting against their act & actions
stop.
act in a way that will cause them
to act the way you want them to act
in accordance with yr/acts & actions:
human acts for human beings

re-act
NOW niggers
& you won't have to
act
false-actions
at
your/children's graves.

Think Black!

FIRST IMPRESSIONS ON A POET'S DEATH

(for Conrad Kent Rivers)

blk/poets die
from
not being
read
& from, maybe,
too much
leg.
some drank
themselves
into
non-poets,
but most
poets who poet
seldom
die
from
overexposure.

TAXES

Income taxes,
        every year—due,
Sales taxes,
        I pay these too.
Luxury taxes,
        maybe—one or two
Black taxes,
        on everything I do.

Mainstream of Society

Irish American, white man too,
    he assimilated into society true.
Italian American, he passed on through,
    assimilation was not easy but he made
        it come true.
German American, white and pure,
    assimilation taken for granted,
        no problems to endure.
Jewish American, am I not white too?
Let me assimilate,
        I can buy my way through.
African American, black man true,
    Instant hate, (a mile away)
    ANNIHILATE
Hell No!
He can't assimilate.

14

"THEY ARE NOT READY"

(the big snow, Chicago, 1967)

They tell me that I am not
fit for society—not because I am black but
because I fight dirty, and at night.
They say that I take advantage of
nature, by using her to help carry out
my mis-deeds of looting shops,
               burning realtors' offices
               and keeping firemen out.

I am not fit for society.

You are society—white anglo-saxon,
               standard setting,
               example setting,
               do it like me pure christian

Americans.

I exist below your standards, America,
yet—I should be satisfied and not burn,
not destroy what is evil to me

There is light, the sun looks on.

I and my children have no shoes, America,
even though there are many shoes around me,
in shoe shops, white shops, day shops that leave the neigh-
borhoods in the evenings
with more shoes than they started with.

This ball of fire—called sun—gives off a
message to those who seek one.
Parking lots are more important than I am.

Think Black!

Night will come.

I know not what a balanced diet is,
you tell me, "nor do the people of India."

The sun is moving towards the horizon.

I can't find work, America, and your reply is,
"you didn't prepare yourself."

The Sun is gone and has left two feet of
aid, white aid.

I DID PREPARE MYSELF.

The day is you,
                    the night is me.

16

No Society!

I am not fit for you and I'll continue
to fight dirty.

AWARENESS

BLACK   PEOPLE   THINK

PEOPLE   BLACK   PEOPLE

THINK   PEOPLE   THINK

BLACK   PEOPLE   THINK—

THINK   BLACK.

Think Black!

2
BLACK PRIDE
(1968)

THE NEW INTEGRATIONIST

I
seek
integration
of
negroes
with
black
people.

STATISTICS

They were married
and lived happily
for a day or two.

She came on her period—
that third day of marriage,
unexpectedly and quite by
surprise, not anticipated
by either one.

They were married
and lived happily
for a day or two.

Two Poems

(from "Sketches from a
Black-Nappy-Headed Poet")

last week
my mother died/
& the most often asked question
at the funeral;
was not of her death
or of her life before death
     but
why was i present
with/out
a
tie on.

i ain't seen no poems stop a .38,
i ain't seen no stanzas break a honkie's head,
i ain't seen no metaphors stop a tank,
i ain't seen no words kill
& if the word was mightier than the sword
pushkin wouldn't be fertilizing russian soil/
& until my similes can protect me from a nightstick
i guess i'll keep my razor
& buy me some more bullets.

23

Black Pride

ONLY A FEW LEFT

(America's Pushkin sings no more
—to Langston Hughes)

The time has come
when bravery
is not he
who is abundant
with heroic deeds
for the
state.
Bravery is that
little black man
over there
surrounded by people
he's talking—
bravery lies in his
words,
he's telling the
truth
they say
he's
a
poet.

THE ONLY ONE

i work days, (9 to 5)
in the front office
of a well-known Chicago
company.
this company is,
"an Equal Opportunity Employer,"
you can look at Me
and tell—everybody does.
my job??
it's unclear, it's new,
created just for me,
last week.
(after a visit from some human righters)
i've been with the company
for 15 years—
at last they gave me my own desk,
(toilet, lunch area & speeches too)
they like me—
(i mind my own business)
i've had, two years of college.
(it didn't matter until now)
They
call me an
EXECUTIVE—
but we,
you and i,
know the
Truth.

25

THE PRIMITIVE

taken from the
shores of Mother Africa,
the savages they thought
we were—
they being the real savages.
to save us. (from what?)
our happiness, our love, each other?
their bible for
our land. (introduction to economics)
christianized us.
roped our minds with:
t.v. & straight hair,
reader's digest & bleaching creams,
tarzan & jungle jim,
used cars & used homes,
reefers & napalm,
european history & promises.
Those alien concepts
of whi-teness,
the being of what
is not.
against our nature,
this weapon called
civilization—
they brought us here—
to drive us mad.
(like them)

CONTRADICTION IN ESSENCE

I
met
a
part
time
re
vo
lu
tion
ist
too—
day

       (natural hair, african dressed,
        always angry, in a hurry &c.)

talk
ing
black
&
sleep
ing
whi
te.

THE DEATH DANCE

(for Maxine)

my empty steps mashed
your face in a mad
rhythm of happiness.
as if i was just learning to
boo-ga-loo.

my mother took the
'b' train to the loop
to seek work & was laughed at by
some dumb, eye-less image maker as
she scored idiot on "your" i. q. test.

i watched mom;
an ebony mind
on a yellow frame.
"i got work son, go back to school."
(she was placed according to her
intelligence into some honkie's kitchen)

i thought & my steps
took on a hip be-bop beat
on your little brain
trying to reach any of
your senseless senses.

mom would come home late
at night & talk sadtalk
or funny sadtalk. she talked
about a pipe smoking sissy
who talked sissy-talk & had
sissy sons who were forever playing
sissy games with themselves
& then she would say,
"son you is a man, a black man."
i was now tap-dancing on your
balls & you felt no pain.

my steps were beating a staccato
message that told of the past 400 years.

the next day mom cried &
sadtalked me. she talked about
the eggs of maggot colored,
gaunt creatures from europe
who came here/put on pants, stopped eating with their
            hands,
stole land, massacred indians,
hid from the sun, enslaved blacks &
thought that they were substitutes
for gods. she talked about a
faggot who grabbed her ass as
she tried to get out of the
backdoor of his kitchen & she said,
"son you is a man, a black man."

the African ballet
was now my guide; a teacher of self &
the dance of a people.
a dance of concept & essence.
i grew.

mom stayed home & the
ADC became my father/in projects without
backdoors/"old grand dad" over
the cries of bessie smith/
until pains didn't pain anymore.

i began to dance dangerous steps,
warrior's steps.
my steps took on a cadence with other blk/brothers
& you could hear the cracking of
gun shots in them & we said that,
"we were men, black men."
i took the 'b' train to the loop &
you SEE me coming,
you don't like it,

---

you can't hide &
you can't stop me.
you will not laugh this time.
you know,
that when i dance again
it will be the
Death Dance.

THE TRAITOR

he wore
a whi
te
shirt
&
bow tie,
a pretty
smile
&
the people called him
doctor.
   (honorary degrees from fisk,
   tenn. state a&i, morehouse &c.)

KA BOMMMM
KA BOMMMM

blood
splattered
his whi
te
shirt
his face
dis-
figured
by shot
gun
pellets
&
his head
fell
against
his
black
cadillac
&

bent
his
"clergy"
sign
toward the
black earth
&
somebody said,
"deal baby—deal."

3
DON'T CRY, SCREAM
(1969)

BLACK POETICS/FOR THE MANY TO COME

The most significant factor about the poems/poetry you will be reading is the *idea*. The *idea* is not the manner in which a poem is conceived but the conception itself. From the *idea* we move toward development & direction (direction: the focusing of yr/idea in a positive or negative manner, depending on the poet's orientation). Poetic form is synonymous with poetic structure and is the guide used in developing yr/idea.

What u will be reading is blackpoetry. Blackpoetry is written for/to/about & around the lives/spiritactions/humanism & total existence of blackpeople. Blackpoetry in form/sound/word usage/intonation/rhythm/repetition/direction/definition & beauty is opposed to that which is now (& yesterday) considered poetry, i.e., whi-te poetry. Blackpoetry in its purest form is diametrically opposed to whi-te poetry. Whereas, blackpoets deal in the concrete rather than the abstract (concrete: art for people's sake; black language or Afro-american language in contrast to standard english, &c.). Blackpoetry moves to define & legitimize blackpeople's reality (*that* which is real to us). Those in power (the unpeople) control and legitimize the negroes' (the realpeople's) reality out of that which they, the unpeople, consider real. That is, to the unpeople the television programs *Julia* and *The Mod Squad* reflect their vision of what they feel the blackman *is* about or *should* be about. So, in effect, blackpoetry is out to negate the negative influences of the mass media; whether it be TV, newspapers, magazines, or some whi-te boy standing on a stage saying he's a "blue eyed soul brother."

Blackpeople must move to where all confrontations with the unpeople are meaningful and constructive. That means that most, if not all, blackpoetry will be *political*. I've often come across black artists (poets, painters, actors, writers, &c.) who feel that they and their work should be apolitical; not realizing that to be apolitical is *to be* political in a negative way for black-folks. There is *no* neutral blackart; either it *is* or it *isn't*, period. To say that one is not political is as dangerous as saying, "by any means necessary," it's an intellectual cop-out, & niggers are copping-out as regularly as blades of grass in a New

England suburb. Being political is also why the black artist is considered dangerous by those who rule, the unpeople. The black artist by defining and legitimizing his own reality becomes a positive force in the black community [just think of the results of Le Roi Jones (Amiri Baraka) writing the lyrics for the music of James Brown]. You see, *black* for the blackpoet is a way of life. And, our totalactions will reflect that blackness & we will be an example for our community rather than another contradictor.

Blackpoetry will continue to define what *is* and what *isn't*. Will tell what is *to be* & how to *be* it (or bes it). Blackpoetry *is* and will continue to be an important factor in culture building. I believe Robert Hayden had culture building in mind when he wrote these lines in an early poem:

> It is time to call the children
> Into the evening quiet of the living-room
> And teach them the legends of their blood.

Blackpoetry is excellence & truth and will continue to seek such. Blackpoetry will move to expose & wipe-out that which is not necessary for our existence as a people. *As a people* is the only way we can endure and blacknation-building must accelerate at top speed. Blackpoetry is Ornette Coleman teaching violin & the Supremes being black again. Blackpoetry is like a razor; it's sharp & will cut deep, not out to wound but to kill the inactive blackmind. Like, my oldman used to pickup numbers and he seldom got caught & I'm faster than him; this is a fight with well defined borders & I know the side I'm ON. See u. Go head, now.

don l. lee

36

she doesn't wear
costume jewelry
& she knew that walt disney
was/is making a fortune off
false eyelashes and that time magazine is the
authority on the knee/grow.
her makeup is total-real.

a negro english instructor called her:
    "a fine negro poet."
a whi-te critic said:
    "she's a credit to the negro race."
somebody else called her:
    "a pure negro writer."
johnnie mae, who's a senior in high school, said:
    "she & langston are the only negro poets we've
    read in school and i understand her."
pee wee used to carry one of her poems around in his
  back pocket;
    the one about being cool. that was befo pee wee
    was cooled by a cop's warning shot.

into the sixties
a word was born. . . . . BLACK
& with black came poets
& from the poet's ball points came:
black doubleblack purpleblack blueblack beenblack was
black daybeforeyesterday blackerthan ultrablack super
black blackblack yellowblack niggerblack blackwhi-te man
blackerthanyoueverbes 1/4 black unblack coldblack clear
black my momma's blackerthanyourmomma pimpleblack fall
black so black we can't even see you black on black in
black by black technically black mantanblack winter
black coolblack 360degreesblack coalblack midnight
black black when it's convenient rustyblack moonblack
black starblack summerblack electronblack spaceman

black shoeshineblack jimshoeblack underwearblack ugly
black auntjimammablack uncleben'srice black williebest
black blackisbeautifulblack i justdiscoveredblack negro
black unsubstanceblack.

and everywhere the
lady "negro poet"
appeared the poets were there.
they listened & questioned
& went home feeling uncomfortable/unsound & so-
      untogether
they read/re-read/wrote & re-wrote
& came back the next time to tell the
lady "negro poet"
how beautiful she was/is & how she had helped them
& she came back with:
      how necessary they were and how they've helped her.
the poets walked & as space filled the vacuum between
      them & the
lady
"negro poet"
u could hear one of the blackpoets say:
      "bro, they been callin that sister by the wrong name."

38

But He Was Cool

or: he even stopped for green lights

super-cool
ultrablack
a tan/purple
had a beautiful shade.

he had a double-natural
that wd put the sisters to shame.
his dashikis were tailor made
& his beads were imported sea shells
   (from some blk/country i never heard of)
he was triple-hip.

his tikis were hand carved
out of ivory
& came express from the motherland.
he would greet u in swahili
& say good-by in yoruba.
wooooooooooooo-jim he bes so cool & ill tel li gent
                    cool-cool is so cool he was un-cooled by
                          other niggers' cool
                    cool-cool ultracool was bop-cool/ice box
                          cool so cool cold cool
                    his wine didn't have to be cooled, him was
                          air conditioned cool
                    cool-cool/real cool made me cool—now
                          ain't that cool
                    cool-cool so cool him nicknamed refrigerator.

cool-cool so cool
he didn't know,
after detroit, newark, chicago &c.,
we had to hip
            cool-cool/super-cool/real cool
      that
to be black
is
to be
very-hot.

dee dee dee dee dee wee weee eeeeee wee we
   deweeeeeeee ee ee ee nig
nig nig nig niggggggggggggggggg cleek cleek cleek
   cleeeeee cleekcleek
rip rip rip rip rip/rip/rip/rip/rip/ripripripripripripripri
   pi pi pi pi pip
bom bom bom bom bom/bom/bom/bombombombom
   bombbombbombbombbombbomb
deathtocleekdeathtocleekdeathtocleekdeathtocleek
   deathtocleekdeathtodeathto
alllllllllllalllllllllll allll llllllll deathtoalllllll l allllllllll
   alllllllleeeeeeee
te te te te te te te/te/te/te/te/te/tetetetetetetetetete
   tetetetetetete:
the paris peace talks, 1968.

40

DON'T CRY, SCREAM

(for John Coltrane/ from a black poet/
in a basement apt. crying dry tears
of "you ain't gone.")

into the sixties
a trane
came/out of the
fifties with a
golden boxcar
riding the rails
of novation.
    blowing
    a-melodics
    screeching,
    screaming,
    blasting—
        driving some away,
        (those paper readers who thought
        manhood was something innate)

        bring others in,
        (the few who didn't believe that the
        world existed around established whi
        teness & leonard bernstein)
music that ached.
murdered our minds (we reborn)
born into a neoteric aberration.
& suddenly
you envy the
BLIND man—
you know that he will
hear what you'll never
see.

your music is like
my head—nappy black/
a good nasty feel with
tangled songs of:
    we-eeeeeeeeee   sing
    WE-EEEeeeeeeeeee   loud &
    WE-EEEEEEE EEEEEEEEEE high
                            with
                            feeling

a people playing
the sound of me when
i combed it. combed at
it.

i cried for billy holiday.
the blues. we ain't blue
the blues exhibited illusions of manhood.
destroyed by you. Ascension into:

    scream-eeeeeeeeeeeeee-ing   sing
    SCREAM-EEEeeeeeeeeeee-ing loud &
    SCREAM-EEEEEEEEEEE EEE-ing long with
                                feeling

we ain't blue, we are black.
we ain't blue, we are black.
    (all the blues did was
    make me cry)
soultrane gone on a trip
he left man images
he was a life-style of
man-makers & annihilator
of attache case carriers.

Trane done went.
(got his hat & left me one)

naw brother,
i didn't cry,
i just—

Scream-eeeeeeeeeeeeee e-ed   sing loud
SCREAM-EEEEEEEEEEEEEEEEEE-ED   & high with
  we-eeeeeeeeeeeeeeeeeeeeee ee   feeling
  WE-E-EEEEEeeeeeeee EEEEEEEE   letting
  WE-EEEEEEEEEEEEEEEEEEEEEEE   yr/voice
  WHERE YOU DONE GONE, BROTHER?   break

it hurts, grown babies
dying. born. done caught me
a trane. steel wheels broken
by popsicle sticks. i went out
& tried to buy a nickle bag
with my standard oil card.

blonds had more fun—
with snagga-tooth niggers
who saved pennies & pop bottles for week-ends
to play negro & other filthy inventions.
be-bop-en to james brown's
cold sweat—these niggers didn't sweat,
they perspired. & the blond's dye came out,
i ran. she did too, with his pennies, pop bottles
& his mind. tune in next week same time same station
for anti-self in one lesson.

to the negro cow-sissies
who did tchaikovsky &
the beatles & live in
split-level homes & had
split-level minds & babies.
who committed the act of
love with their clothes on.
        (who hid in the bathroom to read
        jet mag., who didn't read the chicago
        defender because of the misspelled
        words & had shelves of books by
        europeans on display. untouched. who
        hid their little richard & lightnin'
        slim records & asked: "John who?"

43

instant hate.)
they didn't know any better,
brother, they were too busy getting
into debt, expressing humanity &
taking off color.

SCREAMMMM/we-eeeee/screech/teee   improvise
aheeeeeeeee/screeeeeee/theeee/ee   with
ahHHHHHHHHH/WEEEEEEEE/scrEEE   feeling
    EEEE
we-eeeeeeWE-EEEEEEEEWE-EE-EEEEE
the ofays heard you &
were wiped out. spaced.
one clown asked me during,
my favorite things, if
you were practicing.
i fired on the muthafucka & said,
"i'm practicing."

naw brother,
i didn't cry.
i got high off my thoughts—
they kept coming back,
back to destroy me.

& that BLIND man
i don't envy him anymore
i can see his hear
& hear his heard through my pores.
i can see my me. it was truth you gave,
like a daily shit
it had to come.
        can you scream—brother?   very
        can you scream—brother?   soft

i hear you.
i hear you.

and the Gods will too.

A Poem to Complement other Poems

change.
like if u were a match i wd light u into something beauti-
    ful. change.
change.
for the better into a realreal together thing. change, from
    a make believe
nothing on corn meal and water. change.
change. from the last drop to the first, maxwellhouse
    did. change.
change was a programmer for ibm, thought him was a
    brown computor. change.
colored is something written on southern out-
    houses. change.
greyhound did, i mean they got rest rooms on buses.
    change.
change.
change nigger.
saw a nigger hippy, him wanted to be different.
    changed.
saw a nigger liberal, him wanted to be different.
    changed.
saw a nigger conservative, him wanted to be different.
    changed.
niggers don't u know that niggers are different. change.
a doublechange. nigger wanted a double zero in front of
    his name; a license to kill,
niggers are licensed to be killed. change. a negro: some-
    thing pigs eat.
change. i say change into a realblack righteous aim. like
    i don't play
saxophone but that doesn't mean i don't dig trane.
    change.

change.
hear u coming but yr/steps are too loud. change. even a
    lamp post changes nigger.

change, stop being an instant yes machine. change.
niggers don't change they just grow. that's a change;
    bigger & better niggers.
change, into a necessary blackself.
change, like a gas meter gets higher.
change, like a blues song talking about a righteous to-
    morrow.
change, like a tax bill getting higher.
change, like a good sister getting better.
change, like knowing wood will burn. change.
know the realenemy.
change,
change nigger: standing on the corner, thought him was
                cool. him still
                standing there. it's wintertime, him cool.
change,
know the realenemy.
change: him wanted to be a tv star. him is. ten o'clock
            news.
      wanted, wanted. nigger stole some lemon & lime
         popsicles,
    thought them were diamonds.
change nigger change.
know the realenemy.
change: is u is or is u aint. change. now now change. for
        the better change.
    read a change. live a change. read a blackpoem.
      change. be the realpeople.
    change. blackpoems
will change:

know the realenemy. change. know the realenemy. change
    yr/enemy change know the real
change know the realenemy change, change, know the
    realenemy, the realenemy, the real
realenemy change you're the enemies/change your change
    your change your enemy change
your enemy. know the realenemy, the world's enemy.

know them know them know them the
realenemy change your enemy change your change
      change change your enemy change change
change change your change change change.
your
mind nigger.

HERO

(a poem for brig. general
frederic davison, if he can dig it)

little willie
a hero in
the american tradition.
a blk/hero.
he
received the:
     bronze star: which read "meritorious action,"
        (his momma had to look the word up)
    good conduct medal,
    combat infantry badge,
    purple heart,
    national defense service medal,
    vietnam campaign ribbon,
    & some others i can't even spell.

little willie
a hero in
the american tradition.
a blk/hero.
he
received his medals

p
o
s
t
h
u
m
o
u
s
l
y
.
.
.

48

BLACK SKETCHES

1.
i
was five
when
mom & dad got married
& i
didn't realize that
i
was illegitimate
until i started
school.

2.
i was at
the airport
& had
to use the
men's room
real bad
& didn't have a
dime.

3.
somebody
made a
mistake (they said)
&
sent the
peace corps to
europe.

4.
went to cash
my
1968 tax refund
&
the check bounced;
insufficient funds.

5.
i
read the
newspapers today
&
thought that
everything
was
all right.

6.
nat turner
returned
&
killed
william styron
&
his momma too.

7.
ed brooke
sat at his
desk
crying & slashing
his wrist
because somebody
called him
black.

8.
general westmoreland
was transferred
to the
westside of chicago
&
he lost
there too.

9.
in 1959
my mom
was dead at the
age of
35
& nobody thought it unusual;
not even
me.

10.
in 1963
i
became black
& everyone thought it unusual;
even me.

11.
the american dream:
        nigger bible in
        every hotel;
        iceberg slim (pimp) getting
        next to julia;
        & roy wilkins on
        the mod squad.

BLACKWOMAN:

will define herself. naturally. will
talk/walk/live/& love her images. her
beauty will be. the only way to be is
to be. blackman take her. u don't need
music to move; yr/movement toward her
is music. & she'll do more than dance.

52

THE THIRD WORLD BOND

(for my sisters & their sisters)

they were
blk/revolutionists.
& they often talked
of the third world
& especially of the power
of
china.
   (quoting mao every 3rd word)
they were
revolutionists
& the blk/sisters knew it
& looked,
& wondered
while the brothers/
the revolutionists,
made bonds
with the
3rd world
thru
chinese women.
the sisters waited.
(& wondered when the revolution would start)

53

THE REVOLUTIONARY SCREW

(for my blacksisters)

brothers,
i
under/overstand
the situation:

i mean—
       u bes hitten the man hard
       all day long.
a stone revolutionary, "a full time revolutionary."
       tellen the man how bad u is
       & what u goin ta do
       & how u goin ta do it.

it must be a bitch
to be able to do all that
talken. (& not one irregular breath fr/yr/mouth)
being so
forceful & all
to the man's face (the courage)
& u not even cracken a smile (realman).

i know,
the sisters just don't
understand the
pressure u is under.

&
when u ask for a piece
of leg/
it's not for yr/self
but for
yr/people——it keeps u going
& anyway u is a revolutionary
& she wd be doin
a revolutionary thing.

that sister dug it
from the beginning,
had an early-eye.
i mean
she really had it together
when she said:
        go fuck yr/self nigger.

now
that was
revolutionary.

REFLECTIONS ON A LOST LOVE

(for my brothers who think they are lovers
and my sisters who are the real-lovers)

back in chi/
all the blackwomen
are fine,
super fine.
even the ones who:
     dee bob/de bop/she-shoo-bop
     bop de-bop/dee dee bop/dee-she dee-she-bop
     we-We eeeeeeeeee eeeee/ WEEEEEEE EEEEEEEE
they so fine/
that
when i slide up
to one & say: take it off   sing
             take it off   slow
                take it all off   with feeling

56

& she would say: "if i doos,
         does us think u can groove dad—dy"
& i wd say: "can chitlins smell,
       is toejam black,
       can a poet, poet,
       can a musician, music?"

     weeeee/weeeeeee/de-bop-a-dee-bop
     whooo-bop/dee-bop a-she-bop
as she smiled
& unbuttoned that top button
i sd: take it off   sing
     take it off   slow
       take it all off   with feeling

first the skirt,
then the blouse
& next her wig (looked like she made it herself)

---

next the shoes & then
the eyelashes and jewelry
&
     dee-bop/bop-a-ree-bop/ WOW
the slip
& next the bra (they weren't big, but that didn't scare me
cause i was grooven now): dee/dee-bop-a-she-bop/
      weeeeeEEEEEEEEEE
as she moved to the most important part,
i got up & started to groove myself but my eyes stopped
      me.
first
her stockens down those shapely legs—
followed by black bikini panties, that just slid down
and
i just stood—
& looked with utter amazement as she said: in a deep
      "hi baby—my name is   man-like
       joe sam."   voice

57

A Poem Looking for a Reader

(to be read with a love consciousness)

black is not
all-inclusive,
there are other colors.
color her warm and womanly,
color her feeling and life,
color her a gibran poem & 4 women of simone.
children will give her color
paint her the color of her
man.

most of all color her
love
a remembrance of life
a truereflection
that we
will
move   u will move with
i want
u
a fifty minute call to blackwomanworld:
    hi baby,
    how u doin?
need u.
listening to
young-holt's, *please sunrise, please.*

to give   i'll give
most personal.
what about the other
scenes: children playing in vacant lots,
        or like the first time u knowingly kissed a girl,
        was it joy or just beautifully beautiful.

i
remember at 13
reading chester himes'
cast the first stone and
the eyes of momma when she caught me: read on, son.

how will u come:
    like a soulful strut in a two-piece beige o-rig'i-nal,
    or afro-down with a beat in yr/walk?
how will love come:
    painless and deep like a razor cut
    or like some cheap 75¢ movie;
    i think not.

will she be the woman
other men will want
or
will her beauty be
accented with my name on it?

she will come as she would
want her man to come.
she'll come,
she'll come.
i
never wrote a love letter
but
that doesn't mean
i
don't love.

4

WE WALK THE WAY OF THE NEW WORLD
(1970)

Louder but Softer

Yesterday is not today. What was visible in the old books is *still there*, that's why new ones are written. Yesterday's light was bright and lived suspended within its own energy. Today the only time we see it is by traveling thirty-five thousand feet above the earth at some ridiculous speed; our children will not know the *sun* as we knew it, but will appreciate it more.

We're talking about our children, a survival of a people. A people can't possibly survive if they become something else. The process of change, of reconditioning a people to be something other than themselves, started centuries ago: we used to be blackmen/women (or Africans); now we're known as *negroes*. That movement toward becoming an adjective was not accidental, but carefully planned and immaculately executed to completely rape a people of their culture. Whereas, most of us have become another man's imagination, a reflection of another man's fantasy, a nonentity, a filthy invention. So, in effect we'll be talking about definitions & change. When we say definitions, we mean the present and the past with the proper perspective. Understand that *objectivity* is a *myth* where "one makes judgments in terms of one's culture and in keeping with the cultural values which are a part of his personal and immediate heritage. These cultural values depend for their duration upon the survival of the classes which created them." *Change* is to be that, an on-going process aimed at an ultimate definition of our being. But when we talk about change, we don't mean from *Winston* to *Marlboro*. Actually, we mean from negative to positive, from the creative to the anti-cliché.

63

> *What is meant is that we'll have to move from imitation to initiation; from number one to number first; from the Tonight Show to our own Lenox Avenue where brothers shadowbox with wind because the wind is the only element that will touch them. Check it out, if u ain't scared to venture back.*

Can you believe in yourself? It's not enough to say *I'm Somebody*: we've always known that. The question *is* who/

what? Are you a dead raindrop, reborn in a used coal mine now existing in an oblique closet of your closed mind, only to re-emerge singing "I'm black and I'm proud" while soft peddling *before* the jew into the new self-cleaning ovens. After all, it takes little or no work to be insignificant, but to leave our print, our image on the world, you'll find that twenty-four hours in a day is like seconds in a fast minute.

The rejection of that which was/is ours has been the basis for the acceptance of that which is someone else's. The most effective weapon used against us has been the educational system. We now understand that if *white nationalism* is our teacher, *white nationalism* will be our philosophy regardless of *all* its contradictory and anti-black implications. The educational process is set up largely to preserve that which *is*, not that which necessarily needs to be created, i.e., black nationalism or black consciousness. Thus we find ourselves trying to determine which are the correct answers for future development. Some of the answers will have to be a surprise, but at least we know a surprise is coming.

In the late 60s we existed in a state of *cultural nihilism*, and the destruction that came was mainly against our own in our own. Destruction and misdirection became the overwhelming directives. Positive influences existed in the 60s and before, but their accessibility was limited to the few. So we moved, traveling speedily from one consciousness to another, hoping that our actions would not betray our movement. Blackness as we speak of it today is nothing new; other writers at other times wrote about themselves and their people as we do now. The main difference, if there has to be one, is the audience which the writers directed their voices toward. Black writers—from the first and up into the 60s—have largely (with few exceptions) followed the trend of *being* or becoming "American writers," not *negro* writers but writers who happened to be *negro*. All that is in the process of being erased. We discovered a new psychology. The 60s brought us the work of one Frantz Fanon and his powerful *The Wretched of the Earth* and other books. The Honorable Elijah Muhammad, the prophet of the Nation of Islam, ultimately produced the loudest and clearest voice for the young blacks through El Hajj Malik el Shabazz, better known as Malcolm X, who in turn moved us toward a national consciousness. He heavily influenced a writer who proved to be a consistent bullet in the side of white America—Imamu Amiri Baraka (LeRoi Jones).

> *What does it take to reach you, into you? What is the stimulus that will force you to act; what motivates you in yr inability to conceive of yrself as something special? Will it take the death of a loved one? Will the values you consider valuable have to be destroyed? Is the knowledge of self so painful as to demand that you not accept it and continue to squalor in yr naiveté?*

Culture is the sustaining force of any nation. An effective con game has been played on black people in this country. We've been taught to be anti-black, anti-self. No need in documenting that, for all one has to do is walk in any black neighborhood and if you possess only an ounce of perception, the examples will fly at you. We are the only people in a nation of many people who have consistently let others guide us. We've been so busy taking directions from others that our ability to conceive of ourselves as direction-givers has not had a chance to flourish. However, others—those that traditionally have led us—recognized our revolutionary potential. Harold Cruse puts it this way: "They understood it *instinctively*, (the Negro's white radical allies) and revolutionary theory had little to do with it. What . . . the Negro's allies feared most of all was that this sleeping, dream-walking black giant might wake up and direct the revolution all by himself, relegating his white allies to a humiliating, second-class status. The Negro's allies were not about to tell the Negro anything that might place him on the path to greater power and independence in the revolutionary movement than they themselves had. The rules of the power game meant that unless the American Negro taught himself the profound implications of his own revolutionary significance in America, it would never be taught to him by anyone else." We black people in America are not culturally deprived, but "culturally different"; actually we're products of a dual culture, having the benefits and evils of the dominant WASPS and our own unique Afro-Americanism. Here we are, about thirty million voices (larger than some nations) coming into a new decade, still not fully cognizant of the ultimate reality of our power, if only in sheer numbers.

> "Almost daily, small bands of Jewish arrivals tramp up the gangplank of the Saint Lawrence, the hotel ship acquired by the Danish Refugee Council to house them temporarily...You must understand,' a recently arrived 40 year old female physician said. 'Our world has been shattered. My husband and I...had almost forgotton that we were Jews; we were simply Poles. But then someone denounced us.'...The doctor and her husband—who is also a physician—were...accused of hiding their 'Jewishness.'"
>
> —*Newsweek*, January 12,1970

The theater was Poland, the former homeland of more than three million Jews, reduced to seventy-five thousand after Hitler's Aryan society came into power, and today Poland contains less than fifteen thousand. The year is 1970 and the issue is the same, *race*. We can continue to cloud our direction with meaningless rhetoric and romantic illusions, but when it comes down to the deathwalk, no one will save a people but the people themselves. Let's look at the Jewish and black situations here, since Jews and blacks are among the largest "minority" groups.

How can less than six million American Jews be more effective than Afro-Americans that outnumber them almost five to one? The watchword is culture and a steady "survival motion." The Jewish people have a tradition of togetherness and peoplehood. They've developed a nationalist conscious-ness that's interwoven with their religious reality. They've developed life-giving and life-saving institutions. They've developed the sophistication for survival. If a Jew hates you, you'll never know it; if he plans to kill you, you know even less: Sophistication. They recognized years ago that *Mission Impossible* and *James Bond* are for real. So, how does one

66

compete with such impossible odds without inviting suicide? Simple, yet difficult. You become a nation within a nation. You create and sustain your own identity. In effect, Jewish teachers teach Jewish children, especially in the primary levels; Jewish doctors administer aid to Jewish patients (and others); the Jewish business world services the Jewish community; and each sector continually draws on one another to build that community. Rabbi Zev Segal, head of the country's largest and most influential Jewish Orthodox rabbinical group, estimated that close to one hundred million dollars has been spent annually in the last few years on Jewish educational institutions; he also goes on to say that Jewish education is necessary for the survival of Judaism. Also, he and others *rightly feel* that they face "physical danger" if they as a people cannot remain as a people. Thus, Rabbi Segal feels that the Jewish schools are the "core institutions for Jewish survival and identity."

Elsewhere I've said that if all you are exposed to is Charlie Chan, you'll have a Charlie Chan mentality. A better example is Tarzan. Remember Tarzan grew out of one man's imagination, but because of prevailing anti-black conditions, he immediately became a nation's consciousness. What Tarzan did was not only to turn us away from Africa, but from ourselves. And that's where we are now, still unsure of ourselves, walking after somebody else's dreams, while the only fighting being waged is within the race. The killing of each other is not a test for manhood. But manhood has not been defined. And our survival will ultimately be determined by the will or non-will of black men— it will not be an over night process and we see that our most important asset is the next/and present generation of black college students.

Stop!
Black student after winter vacation on his way back to school (University of America), a part of the Jet set. I wouldn't have noticed him, but he was dressed rather oddly; along with about a five inch natural he had an Indian band around his forehead, with a gold earring in his left ear. A black tiki hung around his neck partially hid under a red and green scarf that loosely covered an orange dashiki that housed a

black turtleneck sweater. His tailor made white bell bottoms were accented by brown buckled cowboy boots while a black slick-haired fur coat rested on his right arm looking like it could bite. Now, here we have a brother that didn't know what he was, an international nigger—you name it, he'll be a part of it. As I approached him, his first words after "What's happnin, baby," were "do you smoke, bro."

Stop!
Time is not new; it must be on our side, we're still here. Send young black brothers and sisters to college and they come home Greeks, talking about they can't relate to the community anymore. So here we have black Alpha Phi Alpha, Delta Sigma Theta, etc., unable to speak Greek, with an obvious non-knowledge of Greek culture—only supported by an ignorance of their own past (or present); only, after four years, to be graduated as some of the best whist players since the Cincinatti Kid who didn't finish high school.

68

Today's black college students fall into two categories: the serious and the unserious. By the unserious I mean the lesser but growing portion of black students who attend today's universities with the attitude that they are "students" and nothing else. Whereas being a "student" implies superficial intellectuality that borders on hipness—that is, being hip enough to be able to quote all the current writers to impress those who are impressed by that; very little study (that's for squares, u a brain anyhow); a lot of partying (with the 3 R's of reading, riting, and rithmetic being replaced with *ripple*, *reefers*, and *rappin'*); and a possession of the attitude that "I got mine, you get yours" or "every person for him/herself," so there exists no real commitment to themselves, or to their people. And lastly we have the student who will say that *all* the courses are irrelevant—not realizing it's going to take some of that irrelevance to put us in a position for survival.

Finally, we have the serious student who is not only committed to one's self, but to one's people. Students who realize that they come to college as black men or women will come out as doctors, lawyers, teachers, historians, writers, etc., who are black, and *not* doctors, lawyers, teachers, historians, writers, etc., who happen to be black. No, you are blackmen and women who are black first and products of your vocation second—therefore understanding our priorities. These are New World students who are in the process of developing the necessary group consciousness, nationalistic consciousness or black consciousness that is absolutely necessary for real development.

You as black students will become the new heroes for our children; will move to replace the pimps, prostitutes and wine-heads who are now viewed as heroes because of no meaningful alternative. A part of your responsibility will be to change a rather complex and growing situation in our communities. Think about it, be for real about realness; it's not for the community to relate to you, you relate to that which you left. The community is still there unchanged. You have changed; the question is how? Please, don't space on us just because you think you're educated now. Don't become the *new* pimps, educated pimps existing as a creation of your own mind, unwilling to share with anyone because you think it's *too deep*. Try us, you may not be as deep as you think you are. Stop romanticizing your existence, stop romanticizing the black revolution. Like Brother Malcolm said, *"if you really understood revolution*, you wouldn't even use the term," or as a sister put it—all the revolutionaries she knew were either *dead* or off quietly planning somewhere. Need I say more?

So we say, move into yr own self, Clean. If we were as together as our music and dancing, we'd be a trip in itself. Can you dig that, if we were as up tight as our dancing and music, we wouldn't have a worry except how to stay new and inventive. For an example, take our music. It is commonly accepted that it is the *only* cultural form that is uniquely American—that is, not an off-shoot of European culture. But still, we don't control our own contributions—the money makers have not been the black musicians but the producers and record companies. What is even worse is that our music is being stolen each and every day and passed off as another's creation—take Tom Jones and Janis Joplin, two white performers who try to sing black. They've not only become rich, while black musicians starve in their own creation, but those two whites, plus others—who are at best poor copies of what they consider black—will after a short period of time become the *standard*. It will get to the point whereas when you speak of *soul* and black music, you will find people automatically thinking of white imitators.

We now find ourselves in the 70s and cannot possibly use the tactics of the 60s. We need innovators and producers of positive change. The older generation's resistance to change is natural; so how do we change without alienating them? How can we reduce if not completely eliminate, the negativism, pettiness and cliquishness that exist and are so damaging? How can we enlarge the narrow choice factor—where in most cases our reality is controlled by Christianity, drugs, or alcohol? How can we create a common consciousness, based on a proven humanism—as we stop trying to prove our humanism to those who are unhuman? It's on us; nobody, nowhere will do it for us.

We Walk the Way of the New World. It's new. As indicated above, we are much louder, but softer, a logical progression, still screaming like a super-sonic wind tuned to a special frequency, but hip enough to realize that even some of those brothers and sisters tuned in will still not hear. The new book is in three parts: *Black Woman Poems*, *African Poems*, and *New World Poems*. Each part is a part of the other: Blackwoman is African and Africa is Blackwoman and they both represent the *New World*.

Actually all three sections are reflections of one blackman—which is to say that the whole book is based upon the direction I feel blackmen should be traveling. When we talk about nationalism, we mean *real* nationalism—that which embodies culture, politics, defense, and economy. We talk about a nationalism that will draw brothers and sisters into self and not alienate them; will answer questions and not only present problems; will build people, not individuals, with leadership qualities. That is, each one of us must possess those qualities of good leadership—a community of leaders, not just followers—who can and will work together. Remember *a leader is not only one that leads but is the best example of that leadership.*

the old musicman   beat into an alien image of nothingness
we
remember you & will not forget
the days, the nights, the weekends
the secret savings for the trip north
or up south. We entered the new cities—
they were not ready for us—
those on the great rivers, the lakes
they were clean then, somewhat pure,
u cd even drink fr/them
& the fish lived there in abundance.
we came by backseat greyhound & special trains
up south came us
to become a part of the pot that was supposed to melt
                        it did and we burned
and we burned into something different & unknown
we acquired a new ethic   a new morality   a new history
and we lost
we lost much   we lost that   that was
we became americans   the best   the real
and blindly adopted america's heroes as our own
our minds wouldn't *function*.
what was wrong?
it couldn't have been the air   it was clean then.

today
from the clouds we look back
seat 16C in the bird with the golden wings.
we came & were different shades of darkness
& we brought our music & dance,
that which wasn't polluted.
we took on the language, manners, mores, dress & religion
of the people with the unusual color.
into the 20th century we wandered rubber-stamped
a poor copy!

71

We Walk the Way of the New World

but the music was ours, the dance was ours, was ours.
& then it was hip—it was hip
to walk, talk & act a certain neighborhoodway,
we wore 24 hr sunglasses & called our woman *baby*,
our woman,
we wished her something else,
& she became that wish.
she developed into what we wanted,
she not only reflected *her*, but reflected us,
was a mirror of our death-desires.
we failed to protect or respect her
& no one else would,
& we didn't understand, we didn't understand.
why,
she be doing the things she don't do.

the sixties brought us black
at different levels, at different colors we searched
while   some of us still pissed into the wind.
we tasted
& turned our heads into a greater vision.
greatness becomes our new values—OOOOOOOO
like   telling yr daughter she's beautiful
& meaning *it*. Vee. Boom   Veeeee   Boom
You going to do it jim! BOOOOOOOOM
You goin ta jump around & startle the world blackman.
goin ta space man, all u got ta do is think space thoughts.
You're *slick* jim, yes you is
slicker than an oil slick, yes you is
just been sliding in the wrong direction. click.
be a *New World* picture.   click,   click.
blackman click blackman click into tomorrow.
Spaced from the old thoughts into
the new. Zooomm. Zoooommmmm Zooommmmmm.
click.
design yr own neighborhoods,   Zoom   it can be,
teach yr own children,   Zoom   Zoom   it can be,

build yr own loop,   Zoom   Zoom   it can be,
feed yr own people.   Zoom   Zoom   it can be,

Watch out world greatness is coming.   click   click.
protect yr own communities,   Zoom   Zoom   it can be.

create *man* blackman. . . .
walk thru the
world
as if You are world itself,   click.
be an extension of everything beautiful & powerful, click
click.
HEY   blackman look like
you'd be named something
like. . . . *earth, sun*
or *mountain.*
Go head, *universe*
Zoommmmmmmm.   Zooommmmmmmmmm
Zoooommmmmmmmmmmmm   click   click.
be it,
blackman.

Soft, Hard, Warm, Sure

soft: the way her eyes view her children.
hard: her hands; a comment on her will.
warm: just the way she is, jim!
sure: as yesterday, she's tomorrow's tomorrow.

74

JUDY-ONE

she's the camera's
subject:
the sun for colored film.

her smile is like
clear light bouncing off
the darkness of the
mediterranean at nighttime.

we all know it,
her smile.
when it's working,
moves like sea water—
always going somewhere

strongly.

MAN THINKING ABOUT WOMAN

some thing is lost in me,
like
the way you lose old thoughts   that
somehow seemed unlost at the right time.

i've not known it or you many days;
we met as friends with an absence of strangeness.
it was the month
that my lines got longer & my metaphors softer.

it was the week   that
i felt the city's narrow breezes rush about
me
looking for a place to disappear
as   i walked the clearway,
sure footed in used sandals screaming to be replaced

your empty shoes (except for used stockings)
partially hidden beneath the dresser
looked at me,
as i sat thoughtlessly   waiting
for your touch.

that day,
as your body rested upon my chest
i saw the shadow of the
window blinds   beam
across the unpainted ceiling
going somewhere
like the somewhere i was going
when
the clearness of yr/teeth,
& the scars on yr/legs stopped me.

your beauty: un-noticed by regular eyes   is
like   a blackbird resting
on a telephone wire   that moves
quietly with the wind.

a southwind.

MARLAYNA

harlem's night upon the world
women there
are drops of algerian sand
with joyeyes overworked to welcome.
beauty flows the curves of her natural,
hangs
on out like saturday night skipping sunday
she walks/moves the natureway.
to a hungry man
she's his watermelon.

Big Momma

finally retired   pensionless
from cleaning somebody else's house
she remained home to clean
the one she didn't own.

in her kitchen where we often talked
the *chicago tribune* served as a tablecloth
for the two cups of tomato soup that went
along with my weekly visit & talkingto.

she was in a seriously-funny mood
& from the get-go she was down, realdown:

>roaches around here are like
>letters on a newspaper
>or
>u gonta be a writer, hunh
>when u gone write me some writen
>or
>the way niggers act around here
>if talk cd kill we'd all be dead.

she's somewhat confused about all this *blackness*
but said that it's good when negroes start putting themselves
first and added: we've always shopped at the colored stores,
>   & the way niggers cut each other up round
>   here every weekend that whiteman don't
>   haveta
>   worry bout no revolution specially when he's
>   gonna haveta pay for it too, anyhow all he's
>   gotta do is drop a truck load of *dope* out
>   there
>   on 43rd st. & all the niggers & yr
>   revolutionaries
>   be too busy getten high & then they'll turn
>   round

and fight each other over who got the
mostest.

we finished our soup and i moved to excuse myself,
as we walked to the front door she made a last comment:
now *luther* i knows you done changed a lots but if
you can think back, we never did eat too much pork
round here anyways, it was bad for the belly.
i shared her smile and agreed.

touching the snow lightly i headed for 43rd st.
at the corner i saw a brother crying   while
trying to hold up a lamp post,
thru his watery eyes i cd see big momma's words.

at sixty-eight
she moves freely, is often right
and when there is food
eats   joyously with her own
real teeth.

MIXED SKETCHES

u feel that way sometimes
wondering:
as a nine year old sister
with burned out hair oddly
smiles at you and sweetly calls you
brother.

u feel that way sometimes
wondering:
as a blackwoman & her six children
are burned out of their apartment with no place
to go & a nappy-headed nigger comes running thru
our neighborhood with a match in his hand cryin
revolution.

u feel that way sometimes
wondering:
seeing sisters in two hundred dollar wigs & suits
fastmoving in black clubs in late surroundings   talking
about late thoughts in late language waiting for late men
that come in with, "i don't want to hear bout nothing black
     tonight."
u feel that way sometimes
wondering:
while eating on newspaper tablecloths
& sleeping on clean bed sheets that couldn't
stop bedbugs   as black children watch their
mothers leave the special buses returning from
special neighborhoods
to clean their "own" unspecial homes.
u feel that way sometimes
wondering:
wondering, how did we survive?

MAN AND WOMAN

(for earnie, 1964)

two baths in one day!
at first i thought that you
just wanted to be clean.
then, u pulled the lights off
& the darkness took me away from my book.
lightly,
i asked about your perfume
u answered,
& added that u splashed it in unknown & strange places
and again lightly,
i asked,
if the perfume was *black*.
at first
our backs touched & we both played sleep.
u turned toward me
& the warmth of yr/blood rushes over me   as
u throw yr/left leg over my left leg
& get dangerous, very dangerous with yr/left hand.
the soul-station comes on automatically
with the aid of yr/right hand.
ike & tina turner are singing "get back"
from yr/touch i flinch and say,
listen to the record, woman!
you don't and i don't   while
"get back" is in rhythm
with the shaking of the bed
that's
mixed with our soft voices
that undoubtedly are heard unconfused through
thin walls

BLACKGIRL LEARNING

she couldn't quote french poetry
that doesn't mean that she ain't read any
probably not
tho gwendolyn brooks & margaret walker
lined her dresser.

she did tell me that
the bible was pure literature
& she showed me her own poetry.
far beyond love verse (& it didn't rhyme)
she wrote about her man.

she said that her man
worshiped her,
he wasn't there.
she told me that he had other things to do:

learning to walk straight.

ON SEEING DIANA GO MADDDDDDDDD

(on the very special occasion of the
death of her two dogs—Tiffany & Li'l
Bit—when she cried her eyelashes off)

a dog lover,
a lover of dogs   in a land where poodles
eat/live cleaner than their masters
& their masters use the colored people
to walk that   which they love, while they
wander in & out of our lives running the world.

(stop! in the name of love, before you break my heart)

u moved with childlike vision
deeper into lassieland to become
the new wonderwoman of the dirty-world
we remember the 3/the three young baaaaad detroiters
of younger years when i & other blacks moved with u
& all our thoughts dwelled on the limits of forget & forgive.

(stop! in the name of love, before you break my heart)

diana,
we left u (back in those un-thinking days)   there
on the dance floor teaching marlon brando the monkey
(the only dance you performed with authority)
we washed our faces anew
as the two of you dreamed a single mind.
diana,
yr/new vision worries me because i,
as once you, knew/know the hungry days   when
our fathers went to ford motor co.,
and our mothers
in the morning traffic to the residential sections of dearborn.
little supreme, only the well fed *forget*.
(stop! in the name of love, before you break. . . .)

ladies & gents we proudly present
the swinging su-premessssss. . . . correction, correction.
ladies & gents we proudly present
diana rossss and the supremes.
and there u stood,
a skinny earthling viewing herself as a mov
ing star. as a mov   ing star u will travel
north by northwest deeper into the ugliness
of yr/bent ego. & for this i/we cannot forgive.

(stop! in the name of love, ...)

u, the gifted voice, a symphony, have now joined the
hippy generation to become unhipped,
to become the symbol of a new aberration,
the wearer of other people's hair.
to become one of the real animals of this earth.
we wish u luck & luckily u'll need it
in yr/new found image of a mov
ing star, a mov   ing star, mov   ing moving
moving on to play
a tooth-pick in a *rin tin tin* mov   ie.

85

FIRST

first.
a woman should be
a woman *first*,
if she's anything.
but
if she's *black*, really *black*
and a woman
that's special, that's
realspecial.

WE'RE AN AFRICANPEOPLE

WE'RE an Africanpeople
hard-softness burning black.
the earth's magic color our veins.
an Africanpeople are we;
burning blacker softly, softer.

A POEM FOR A POET

(for brother Mahmood Darweesh)

read yr/exile
i had a mother too,
& her death will not be
talked of around the world.
like you,
i live/walk a strange land.
my smiles are real but seldom.

our enemies eat the same bread
and their waste
(there is always waste)
is given to the pigs,
and then they consume the pigs.

Africa still has sun & moon,
has clean grass & water u can see thru;
Africa's people talk to u with their whole faces,
and their speech comes like drumbeats,
            comes like drumbeats.

our enemies eat the same bread
and the waste from their greed
will darken your sun and hide your moon,
will dirty your grass and misuse your water.
your people will talk with unchanging eyes
and their speech will be slow & unsure & overquick.

Africa, be yr/own letters
or
all your people will want cars
and there are few roads.
you must eat yr/own food
and that which is left,
continue to share in earnest.

Keep your realmen; yr/sculptors
yr/poets, yr/fathers, yr/musicians, yr/sons, yr/warriors.
Keep your truemen of the darkskin,
a father guides his children,
keep them & they'll return your wisdom,
and
if you must send them,   send them
the way of the Sun
as to make them

blacker.

Change is Not Always Progress

(for Africa & Africans)

Africa.

don't let them
steal
your face   or
take your circles
and make them squares.

don't let them
steel
your body   as to put
100 stories of concrete on you
so that you
          arrogantly
scrape
the

sky.

Knocking Donkey Fleas off a Poet from the Southside of Chi

(for brother ted joans)

a worldman.
with the careful eye; the deep look, the newest look.
as recent & hip as the uncola being sipped by
thelonious monk
jackie-ing it down to little *rootie tootie's*.

he's a continent jumper,
a show-upper, a neo-be-bopper.
he's the first u see the last to flee,
the homeboy in African land;
with an inner compass of the rightway.
at times he's the overlooked   like
a rhinoceros in a bird bath.

the sound of his trumpet is the true *off minor*.
to hear him tell it: *bird* is alive, blacks must colonize europe,
                jazz is a woman & I did, I was, I am.
& I believe him.

he's younger than his poems
& old as his clothes,
he's badder than bad: him so bad he cd take a banana from a
                gorilla, pull a pork chop out of a lion's
                buttocks   or debate the horrors of
                war with spiro agnew with his mouth
                closed.

a worldman,
a man of his world.

ted joans is the tan of the sun; the sun's tan.
a violent/peace
looking for a piece.
he'll find it   (in the only place he hasn't been)

We Walk the Way of the New World

among the stars,   that star.
the one that's missing.
last seen
walking slowly across Africa
bringing the rest of the world with it.

CHANGE

change.
create a climate for
change.
yesterday's weather has been un-
changeable.
there is a young dark storm coming;
has   nappy-hair.

SUN HOUSE

(a living legend)

his fingers leaned
forcefully against the neck
of a broken gin bottle
that
rubbed gently on
the steel strings of a borrowed guitar.

the roughness of his voice
is only matched by his immediate
presence that is lifted into
life with lonely words: "is u is or is u ain't
         my baby, i say,
         is u is or is u ain't
         my baby, if u ain't
         don't confess it now."

to himself he knew the answers
& the answers were amplified
by the sharpness of the broken bottle
that gave accent
to the muddy music as it screamed
& scratched the unpure lines
of our many faces,
while our bodies jumped to the sounds of

mississippi.

ONE SIDED SHOOT-OUT

(for brothers fred hampton & mark clark,
murdered 12/4/69 by chicago police at
4: 30 AM while they slept)

only a few will really understand:
it won't be yr/mommas or yr/brothers & sisters or even me,
we all think that we do   but we don't.
it's not *new*   and
under all the rhetoric the seriousness is still not serious.
the national rap deliberately continues, "wipe them niggers
          out."
(no talk do it, no talk do it, no talk do it, notalk notalknotalk
          do it)

& we.
running circleround getting caught in our own cobwebs,
in the same old clothes, same old words, just new adjectives.
we will order new buttons & posters with: "remember fred"
          & "rite-on mark."
& yr/pictures will be beautiful & manly with the deeplook/
          the accusing look
to remind us
to remind us that suicide is not black.

the questions will be asked & the answers will be the new
          clichés.
but maybe,
just maybe we'll finally realize that "revolution" to the real
          world
is international 24hours a day and that 4: 30AM is like
          12:00 noon,
it's just darker.
but the evil can be seen if u look in the right direction.

were the street lights out?
did they darken their faces in combat?
did they remove their shoes to *creep* softer?
could u not see the whi-te of their eyes,
the whi-te of their deathfaces?
didn't yr/look-out man see them coming,   coming,   coming?
or did they turn into ghostdust and join the night's fog?

it was mean.
& we continue to call them "pigs" and "muthafuckas"
        forgetting what all
black children learn very early: "sticks & stones may break
                        my bones but names can
                        never hurt me."
it was murder.
& we meet to hear the speeches/the same, the duplicators.
they say that which is expected of them.
to be instructive or constructive is to be unpopular (like: the
            leaders only
sleep when there is a watchingeye)
but they say the right things at the right time, it's like a
  stageshow:
only the entertainers have changed.
we remember bobby hutton.   the same,   the duplicators.

the seeing eye should always see.
the night doesn't stop the stars
& our enemies scope the ways of blackness in three bad
            shifts a day.
in the AM their music becomes deadlier.
this is a game of dirt.

only blackpeople play it fair.

For Black People

(& negroes too. a poetic statement on black existence in america
with a view of tomorrow. all action takes place on the continent of
north america. these words, imperfect as they may be, are from
positive images received from gwendolyn brooks, hoyt w. fuller,
imamu baraka & joe goncalves.)

I. IN THE BEGINNING

state street was dead, wiped out.
ghetto expressways were up-lifted
and dropped on catholic churches.
all around us trees were being up rooted.
and flung into the entrances of bars, taverns & houses
of prostitution
lake meadows and prairie shores
passed out faces with human bodies of
black & whi-te mixed together, like salt & pepper,
—in concrete silence.
though deceased, some of the bodies still had smiles
—on their faces.
BONG BONG BONG BONG BONG BONG BONG
    BONG
IT STARTED LAST SUNDAY.
for some unknown reason all the baptist ministers—
    told the truth.
it was like committing mass suicide.
it was cold, mid-december, but the streets were hot.
the upward bound programs had failed that year.
the big bombs had been dropped, harlem &
    newark were annihilated.
another six million had perished and now
the two big men were fighting for universal survival.
the scene was blow for blow at the corner of 59th & racine,
right in front of the "Lead Me By the Hand"

We Walk the Way of the New World

storefront church.
J.C. the blue eyed blond, had the upper hand for his
opponent, Allah, was weakening because of the strange—
    climate.
ahhhhh, ohoooooo, ahhaaaaa, ahhhaaaeeEEEE
in a bedroom across the street a blk/woman tearlessly
cries as she spread her legs, in hatred, for her landlord—
    paul goldstein.
(her children will eat tonight)
her brothers, boy-men called negroes, were off hiding
in some known place biting their nails & dreaming of
    whi-te virgins.
that year negroes continued to follow blind men whose
    eye-vision was less than their own & each morning
    negroes woke up a little deader.
the sun was less than bright, air pollution acted as a filter.
colored people were fighting each other knowingly
and little niggers were killing little niggers.
the "best" jobs were taken by colored college graduates
who had earned their degrees in a four-year course of
    self-hatred with a minor in speech.
negroes religiously followed a blondhairedblueeyedman
    and no one forced them
whi-te boys continued to laugh and take blk/women.
negroes were unable to smile & their tears were dry. They
    had no eye-balls.
their sisters went to strangers' beds cursing them.
that year negroes read styron, mailer, joyce and rimbaud.
last year it was bellow, wallace, sartre & voznesensky
(yevtushenko was unpoetic).
somebody said that there was no such thing as black lit-
erature & anyway we all knew that negroes didn't write,
except occasional letters to the editor.
niggers 3 steps from being shoeshine boys were dressing
and talking like william buckley jr.—minus the pencil.
their heroes danced unclothed out of greek mythology.
janis smyth & claude iforgethislastname often quoted pas-

sages from antigone (pronounced anti-gone).
the pope, all perfumed down—smelling like a french sissy,
watched 59th and racine from st. peters with a rosary
in his hand:
hell mary full of grace the lord is with thee.
hell mary full of grace the lord is with thee.
hell mary full of grace the lord was with thee.
blk/poets were not citizens & were being imprisoned and put
to death.
whi-te boys remained our teachers & taught the people
of color
how to be negroes and homosexuals.
some invisible fiction writer continued to praise the poverty
program & is now being considered for "negro writer
in residence" at johnson city, texas.
a blind negro poet compared himself with yeats
not knowing that he, himself, was a "savage side show."
all this happened in the beginning
and the beginning is almost the end.

II. TRANSITION AND MIDDLE PASSAGE

gas masks were worn as were side-arms.
the two nations indivisible & black people began to believe
     in themselves.
muhammad ali remained the third world's champ &
     taught the people self-defense.
blk/poets were released from prison & acted as consultants
     to the blk/nation.
there were regular napalm raids over the whi-te house.
college trained negroes finally realized that they weren't
     educated and expressed sorrow for losing their
     virginity in europe.
the urban progress centers were transformed into hospitals
     & the records were used for toilet paper.
the room was whi-te & the blacks entered only to find
     that the two colors wouldn't mix.
deee-bop a bop bop, dee dee abop, bop-o-bop dee dee,
     wee, WEEEEEE.
willie johnson, all processed down, was noticeably driving
down cottage grove in a gold & black deuce & a quarter;
hitting the steering wheel at 60 degrees off center, with
his head almost touching the right window. willie, dressed
in a gold ban-lon that matched his ride, slowly moved his
left foot to his dual stereo that coolly gave out jerry
butler's: "never gone ta give you up."
while miss wilberforce, alias miss perm of 1967, tried
to pass him on his right side in her pine-yellow 287 must-
ang with the gas tank always on full. dressed in a two-
piece beige marshall field's o-ri-ginal, miss perm with hair
flowing in the wind was nodding her head to the same tune:
    "never gone ta give you up."
both, the stang & the deuce hit the corner of 39th & cottage
at the same time; and as if somebody said; "black is
beautiful," miss perm and processed-down looked at each
other with educated eyes that said:
                 i hate you.

100

that year even lovers didn't love.

whi-te boys continued to take blk/women to bed; but they
ceased to wake up alive.

this was the same year that the picture "guess who's
coming to dinner" killed spencer tracy.

negro pimps were perpetual victims of assassination &
nobody cried.

Amiri Baraka wrote the words to the blk/national anthem &
pharoah sanders composed the music. tauhid became
our war song.

an alive wise man will speak to us, he will quote du bois,
nkrumah, coltrane, fanon, muhammad, trotter and himself.
we will listen.

chicago became known as negro-butcher to the world &
no one believed it would happen, except the jews—
the ones who helped plan it.

forgetting their own past—they were americans now.

eartha kitt talked to nbc about blk/survival; receiving
her instructions from the bedroom at night.

blk/people stopped viewing TV & received the new
messages from the talking drum.

dope pushers were given overdoses of their own junk
& they died. no one cried.

united fruit co. & standard oil were wiped out & whi-te
people cried.

at last, the president could not control our dreams
and the only weapon he could threaten us with
was death.

III. THE END IS THE REAL WORLD

it is a new day and the sun is not dead.
Allah won the fight at 59th & racine and his sons are not
   dead.
blk/poets are playing & we can hear. marvin x & askia
muhammad toure walk the streets with smiles on their
faces. i join them. we talk & listen to our own words.
we set aside one day a year in remembrance of whi-teness.
             (anglo-saxon american history day)
the air is clean. men & women are able to love.
legal holidays still fall in february: the 14th and 23rd*
all the pigs were put to death, the ones with men-like
   minds too.
men stopped eating each other and hunger existed only in
   history books.
money was abolished and everybody was rich.
every home became a house of worship & pure water runs
   again.
young blk/poets take direction from older blk/poets &
   everybody listens.
those who speak have something to say & people seldom
   talk about themselves.
those who have something to say wait their turn & listen to
   their own message.
the hip thing is not to be cool & get high but to be cool &
   help yr/brother.
the pope retired & returned the land & valuables his
   organization had stolen under the guise of religion.
Allah became a part of the people & the people knew &
   loved him as they knew and loved themselves.

*Birth dates of Frederick Douglass and W. E. B. Du Bois

the world was quiet and gentle and beauty came back.
people were able to breathe.
blk/women were respected and protected & their actions
proved deserving of such respect & protection.
each home had a library that was overused.
the blackman had survived.
he was truly the "desert people."
there were black communities, red communities, yellow
      communities and a few whi-te communities that were
      closely watched.
there was not a need for gun control.
there was no need for the word peace for its
      antonym had been removed from the vocabulary.
like i sd befo
the end is the real world.

July, 1968

SEE SAMMY RUN IN THE WRONG DIRECTION

(for the ten *negro* editors representing n.n.p.a.
who visited occupied *Palestine* [known as Israel]
on a fact finding trip, but upon their return—
reported few facts, if any.)

we know others.
are u others, or are u inbetweens?
imitation imitations. like junior sammy davises
kissing the wailing wall
in the forgotten occupied country.
his top lip stuck
& in a strange land he hollered for his momma
not being jewish
naturally
she was off some place   being herself.

with his bottom lip free
he talked to himself as his bad eye
saw the wall coming
even at the deathmoment he tried to steal
the newsong.
afterall
he was just a jewish boy
who happened to be negro.

the deathmoment coming, the wall.
& the jewishnegro tried his infamous impersonations:
      cagney, sullivan, bogart, martin,
      lewis, durante, lawford, sinatra,
      with tom jones & janis joplin both
      singing, "i wish i was black."

but the good eye saw
the realdeath   the certaindeath
while the brainmessages charged the body
for the impression of impressions

& sammy tried but his blood was   gone
            his inner self was   gone
            his hair turned   back

and
he began to really see
as the wall came,
it failed and   he failed   to do
an impression of a

blackman.

105

We Walk the Way of the New World

1.
we run the dangercourse.
the way of the stocking caps & murray's grease.
(if u is modern u used duke greaseless hair pomade)
jo jo was modern/an international nigger
                    born: jan. 1, 1863 in new york, mississippi.
his momma was mo militant than he was/is
jo jo bes no instant negro
his development took all of 106 years
& he was the first to be stamped "made in USA"
where he arrived bow-legged a curve ahead of the 20th
            century's new weapon: television.
which invented, "how to win and influence people"
& gave jo jo his how/ever look: how ever u want me.

we discovered that with the right brand of cigarettes
that one, with his best girl,
cd skip thru grassy fields in living color
& in slow-motion: Caution: niggers, cigarette smoking
                    will kill u & yr/health.
& that the breakfast of champions is: blackeyed peas & rice.
& that God is dead & Jesus is black and last seen on 63rd
            street in a gold & black dashiki, sitting in a pink
            hog speaking swahili with a pig-latin accent.
& that integration and coalition are synonymous,
& that the only thing that really mattered was:
      who could get the highest on the least or how to expand
      & break one's mind.

in the coming world
new prizes are
to be given
we *ran* the dangercourse.
now, it's a silent walk/a careful eye

jo jo is there
to his mother he is unknown
(she accepted with a newlook: what wd u do if someone
        loved u?)
jo jo is back
& he will catch all the new jo jos as they wander in & out
and with a fan-like whisper say: you ain't no
                                   tourist
                                   and Harlem ain't for
                                   sight-seeing, brother.

2.
Start with the itch and there will be no scratch. Study
        yourself.
Watch yr/every movement as u skip thru-out the southside of
        chicago.
be hip to yr/actions.

our dreams are realities
traveling the nature-way.
we meet them
at the apex of their utmost
meanings/means;
we walk in cleanliness
down state st/or Fifth Ave.
& wicked apartment buildings shake
as their windows announce our presence
as we jump into the interior
& cut the day's evil away.

We walk in cleanliness
the newness of it all
becomes us
our women listen to us
and learn.
We teach our children thru
our actions.

We'll become owners of the   New World
the New World.
will run it as unowners
for
we will live in it too
& will want to be remembered
as   realpeople.

MOVE UN-NOTICED TO BE NOTICED:
A NATIONHOOD POEM

move, into our own, not theirs
into our.
they own it (for the moment): the unclean world, the
                    polluted space, the un-censored
                    air, yr/foot steps as they run
                    wildly in the wrong direction.
move, into our own, not theirs
into our.
move, you can't buy own.
own is like yr/hair (if u let it live); a natural extension of
        ownself.
own is yr/reflection, yr/total-being; the way u walk, talk,
            dress and relate to each other is *own.*
own is you,
cannot be bought or sold: can u buy yr/writing hand
                    yr/dancing feet, yr/speech,
                    yr/woman (if she's real),
                    yr/manhood?
own is ours.
all we have to do is   *take it,*
take it the way u take from one another,
        the way u take artur rubenstein over thelonious monk,
        the way u take eugene genovese over lerone bennett,
        the way u take robert bly over imamu baraka,
        the way u take picasso over charles white,
        the way u take marianne moore over gwendolyn
            brooks,
        the way u take *inaction* over *action.*

move. move to act.   act.
act into thinking and think into action.
try to think. think.   try to think think think.
try to think. think (like i said, into yr/own) think.
try to think. don't hurt yourself, i know it's new.

---

try to act,
act into thinking and think into action.
can u do it, hunh? i say hunh, can u stop moving like a drunk
    gorilla?

                ha ha   che che
                ha ha   che che
                ha ha   che che
                ha ha   che che
move
what is u anyhow: a professional car watcher, a billboard for
    nothingness, a sane madman, a reincarnated clark
    gable?
either you is or you ain't!

the deadliving
are the worldmakers,
the image breakers,
the rule takers: blackman can you stop a hurricane?

"I remember back in 1954 or '55, in Chicago, when we had
13 days without a murder, that was before them colored
people started calling themselves *black*."
move.
move,
move to be moved,
move into yr/ownself, Clean.
Clean, u is the first black hippy i've ever met.
why u bes dressen so funny, anyhow, hunh?
i mean, is that u Clean?
why u bes dressen like an airplane, can u fly,
i mean,
will yr/blue jim-shoes fly u,
& what about yr/tailor made bell bottoms, Clean?
can they lift u above madness,
turn u into the right direction,
& that red & pink scarf around yr/neck what's that for Clean,
hunh? will it help u fly, yeah, swing, swing   ing swing
    swinging high above telephone wires with dreams
    of this & that and illusions of trying to take bar-b-q

ice cream away from lion minded niggers who
didn't even know that *polish* is more than a
sausage.
"clean as a tack,
rusty as a nail,
haven't had a bath
since columbus sail."

when u goin be something real, Clean?
like yr/own, yeah, when u goin be yr/ownself?

the deadliving
are the worldmakers,
the image breakers,
the rule takers: blackman can u stop a hurricane, mississippi
couldn't.
blackman if u can't stop what mississippi couldn't, *be it. be it.*
blackman be the wind, be the win, the win, the win, win win:

woooooooooowe boom boom   woooooooooowe bah
woooooooooowe boom boom   woooooooooowe bah
if u can't stop a hurricane, be one.
woooooooooowe boom boom   woooooooooowe bah
woooooooooowe boom boom   woooooooooowe bah

be the baddddest hurricane that ever came, a black
                    hurricane.
woooooooooowe boom boom   woooooooooowe bah
woooooooooowe boom boom   woooooooooowe bah
the badddest black hurricane that ever came, a black
                    hurricane named Beulah,
go head Beulah, do the hurricane.
woooooooooowe boom boom   woooooooooowe bah
woooooooooowe boom boom   woooooooooowe bah
move
move to be moved from the un-moveable,
into our own, yr/self is own, yrself is own, own yourself.
go where you/we go, hear the unheard and do,
do the undone, do it, do it, do it *now*, Clean

We Walk the Way of the New World

and tomorrow your sons will
be alive to praise
you.

112

CHANGE-UP

change-up,
let's go for ourselves
both cheeks are broken now.
change-up,
move past the corner bar,
let yr/spirit lift u above that quick high.
change-up,
that tooth pick you're sucking on was
once a log.
change-up,
and yr/children will look at us differently
than we looked at our parents.

5
Directionscore
(1971)

Positives: for Sterling Plumpp

can u walk away from ugly,
will u sample the visions of yr self,
is ugly u? it ain't yr momma, yr woman,
>the brother who stepped on yr alligator shoes,
>yr wig wearen believen in Jesus grandmomma, or
>the honda ridden see-thru jump suit wearen brother.

yeah,
caught u upsidedown jay-walking across europe
to catch badness running against yr self.
didn't u know u were lost brother?
confused hair with blackness
thought u knew it before the knower did,
didn't u know u lost brother?
thought u were bad until u ran up against BAD:
Du Pont, Ford, General Motors   even the latest
Paris fashions: & u goin ta get rich off dashikis before Sears.
didn't u know u were lost brother?

beat laziness back into the outside,
run the mirror of ugliness into its inventors,
will u sample the visions of yr self?
quiet   like the way u do it soft spoken   quiet
quiet   more dangerous than danger a new   quiet
quiet   no name quiet no number quiet pure   quiet
quiet   to pure to purer.

a full back clean-up man   a black earthmover
my main man
change yr name like the wind
blow in any direction catch righteousness,
u may have ta smile at the big preacher in town,
thats alright organize in the church washroom,
trick the brother into learning—

Directionscore

be as together as a 360 computer:
      can u think as well as u talk,
      can u read as well as u drink,
      can u teach as well as u dress?
sample the new visions of yr work brother & smile
we'll push Du Bois like they push the racing form.

yr woman goin ta look up to u,
yr children goin ta call u hero,
u my main nigger
the somethin like the somethin
u ain't suppose   *to be.*

WITH ALL DELIBERATE SPEED
(for the children of our world)

in july of 19 somethin
the year of the "love it or leave it" stickers,
a pink sharecropper former KKK   now
a wallacite pro-bircher
undercover minuteman
living in n.y. city   as
a used hardhat flag waving,
beer belly torn undershirt wearen
hawk.

is also
an unread bible carrying preacher
& secret draft dodger from WW 2
who
went to washington d.c.
at government's expense   for
the 1970 honor america day   and
support our boys in viet nam
also
took time out to find
& wildly   slap   slap   slap   slap
one
B.A., M.A., LLD., N.E.G.R.O.,
supreme court justice in the mouth   and
with all deliberate speed
went home to alabama
to brag about
it.

TO BE QUICKER
FOR BLACK POLITICAL PRISONERS
ON THE INSIDE & OUTSIDE—REAL

(to my brothers & sisters of OBAC)

climb ape mountain backwards
better than the better u thought u had to be better than
jump clean.   cleaner.
jump past lightning into field-motion, feel-motion, feel mo
feel mo than the world thought u capable of feelin.
cd do it even fool yr momma, jim! fool yrself, hunh—

goin ta be cleaner,   hunh.
goin ta be stronger,   hunh.
goin ta be wiser,   hunh.
goin ta be quick to be quicker   *to be.*

quick to be whats needed to be   whats needed:
quicker than enemies of the livingworld,
quicker than cheap smiles of a cadillac salesman,
quicker than a dead junky talkin to the wind,
quicker than super-slick niggers sliding in the opposite,
quicker than whi-te-titty-new-left-what's-left suckin niggers,
quicker to be quick, to be quick.

u wise brother.
u wiser than my father was   when he
talked the talk   he wasn't suppose to talk.

quicker to be quick, to be:

a black-African-fist slapping a wop-dope pusher's momma,
a hospital a school anything workin to save us to pull us
closer to Tanzania to Guinea to Harlem to the West Indies to
closer to momma to sister to brother closer to closer to
FRELIMO to Rastafory to us to power to running run to build
to controllifelines to Ashanti to music to life to Allah closer
to Kenya to the black world to the rays of anti-evil.

climb ape mountain backwards   brother
feel better than the better u thought was better
its yr walk brother,
lean a little, cut the smell of nasty.
jump forward into the past
to bring back

goodness.

AN AFTERWORD: FOR GWEN BROOKS

(the search for the new-song begins with the old)

knowing her is not knowing her.

is not
autograph lines or souvenir signatures & shared smiles,
is not
pulitzers, poet laureates or honorary degrees
you see   we ordinary people
just know
ordinary people

to read gwen is to be,
to experience her in the *real*
is the same, she is her words,   more
like a fixed part of the world   is there
quietly penetrating   slow
reminds us of a willie kgositsile love poem   or
issac hayes singing *one woman.*

still
she suggests more;
have u ever seen her home?
it's an idea of her: a brown wooden frame
trimmed in dark gray with a new screen door.
inside: looks like the lady owes everybody on the southside
               nothing but books momma's books.
her home like her person is under-fed and small.

gwen:
pours smiles of african-rain
a pleasure well received among uncollected garbage cans
and heatless basement apartments.
her voice the needle for new-songs
plays unsolicited messages: poets, we've all seen
poets. minor poets ruined by
minor fame.

MWILU/OR POEM FOR THE LIVING

(for charles & Latanya)

jump bigness upward
like u jump clean   make everyday the weekend
& work like u party.

u justice brother, in the world of the un
just be there when wanted when needed when
yr woman calls yr name Musyoka* when yr son
wants direction strength give it, suh. suh
we call u strength suh, call u whatever.

be other than the common   build the sky
work;
study the bringers of anti-good,
question Jesus in the real,
& walk knowledge like you walk unowned streets, brother.
read like u eat   only betta   betta Musemi,*
Musemi be yr name   run emptiness into its givers
& collect the rays of wisdom.
there's goodness in yr eyes giver,   give.
yr wind is chicago-big, Kitheka: Afrikan forest right-wind
running waking dullness of the night-thinkers in the wrong.

why we rather be evil, momma?
why we ain't togatha, Rev. Cleopelius?
why we slide under with tight smiles of forgiveness, Judas?
why our women want to be men, Amana?
why our men want to be somethin other, Muthusi?
what's goin ta make us   us, Kimanthi?
why we don't control our school, Mr. Farmer?
why we don't have any land, big negro?
why we against love, pimps?

123

FRELIMO* in chicago talkin to the *stones*
hear what the real rocks have ta say.
be strange in the righteous
move away dumbjunkies leaning into death:
    never Muslim eating pig sandwiches never
    never listerine breath even cuss proper never
    never u ignorant because *smart* was yr teacher never
    never wander under wonder fan-like avenues   never
    never *will be never* as long as never teaches   never.
snatching answers from the blue   while
giving lip-service   before imitating yr
executers.

jump bigness upward
Impressions puttin Fanon to music & sing like
black-rubbermen over smoked garbage cans with
music of a newer year among stolen nights in
basement corners meet u in the show, baby
just below the health food sign by sam's with
clean water over oiled fish as miniskirted sisters
wear peace symbols supporting the Israelis as
unfeeling as the *east india company*. wdn't dance
to the words of Garvey on pill hill eatin cornbread
with a fork in a see-thru walking suit while running
the fields of crazy while teaching the whi-te boy
the hand-shake. would sell yr momma if somebody wd buy
       her
hunh. roach-back challenge space after un-eaten spit.
goin ta still call u brother,
goin to still call u sister too, hunh.
brother, sister
young lovers of current doo-wops
rake cleanliness brother:

& study unwritten words of manhood.
young lovers of current doo-wops
what's yr new name sister:
reflect the goodness of yr man.
like the way u talk to each other,   like it.

---

the way yr voices pull smiles
u+u=2 over 2 which is 1.

raised higher than surprised quietness
kiss each other   and
touch the feel of secret words
while we all walk in the
shadows of greatness.

---

*The African names used are from the Swahili language of central &
    east Africa
Mwilu (Mwi-lu)—of black; likes black
Musyoka (Mu-syo-ka)—one who always returns
Musomi (Mu-so-mi)—scholarly; reads; studies
Kitheka (Ki-*the*-ka)—wanderer of the forest
Amana (A-ma-na)—peacefulness; serenity; feminine
Kimanthi (Ki-ma-*nthi*)—one who searches for freedom, wealth, love
FRELIMO—Freedom fighters from Mozambique (southeast Africa)

Directionscore

6
BOOK OF LIFE
(1973)

DISCOVERING THE TRAITORS

This work comes at a difficult time in our lives. Comes at a period when we, as a race, are under much weight and can smell and feel the call of death in our very midst. This is odd. It is odd to be so concerned about death when we know deep inside that life is for living, is for developing, is for building, is for creating, is for loving. Yet today, August 27, 1973 our smiles are still few—yet we do smile because we know too that we must not, if possible, convey the death to our children. We know that we must *seem* and *be* the promise of tomorrow. We know that we must be the music of days coming. We know that we must dance while we prepare to fight.

Time moves and passes many of us by, leaving both the closed and open eyed, leaving the hanger-ons and the pimps of the race. And, the question remains: how do we, *as a people*, regain our rightful place in the world? Good question, difficult question, and there are other good and difficult questions that must be asked if we are to get answers and begin to prepare. We came as lovers worldwide not understanding *what it ain't*. We *attack the anti* rather than *be the pro*. We seek answers in the enemy's den and dare to lie to our mothers about our secret associations. The time for honesty has passed—it was about sixty years ago that negroes betrayed each other for recognition from the enemies of the world. It didn't get us anything then and it will not get us anything now. Except—certain defeat and disrespect. Yes, we came as lovers and left as killers. Enemies to ourselves. We have become our own worst enemy—a cliché, yes, but oh so true. We revolve around each other like aged boxers going for a last TKO. Our exercise now is leaning out third floor windows observing our part of the world speed by us; our exercise now is the daily ritual of putting on false eyelashes. Tell me, talk to me—why are we so immobile in a world of mobility? *We must question our powerlessness.* We must recognize the necessity for collective movement among so many *individuals*. It may be that the most individual of the world's individuals is the *negro*. This speaks to our defenselessness, speaks to our ignorance, our stupidity.

Any act of giving is an act of receiving. We are not a weak people: we're just weakened at this moment. We'll find strength in each other—we'll reinforce each other, thus giving and receiving simultaneously. Togetherness at a revolutionary level. We are a world people. We black people exist in abundance worldwide and must begin to forge a *black world unity*. Black world unity is the only vehicle that will enable us to survive *white world unity*. However, we fall into many traps and unknowingly play games with our children's lives and mistakenly call these games jobs, positions, status, security, etc. The only job that is mandatory is working for the race. The only security we have is each other, working for the race together. And as long as a people do not know these basic facts, they will not function as a people and will remain enslaved as a people, not as individuals.

This is obvious to some. The poets know it. But the poets have become the traitors. The poets have become comfortable and published. The poets now talk of "private lives" and "my business." The poets make best seller records and sip coffee with the editors of America's leading publishing houses. They talk of the best for "my child" and about going to the Bahamas to write the next book. They too now talk of making it and getting over. The poets have become traitors. And
when you can't trust the poets, who is left?
After the fact comes the expected,
After the act come the poets and poems,
After the killing come the singer and songs,
After the funeral come the pimps in disguise.
What does U.N.I.T.A.* do with the poets who betray them?
What does P.A.I.G.C.** do with the poets and artists who
betray the people?
What did the Vietnamese do about them?
What type of re-education do the poets receive in China and
Guinea?

Yes, we know, but we are not prepared for that here in the land of the "artists." And really are the poets worth such attention? Probably not. But when you're so close to the air, you must breathe it. Life comes in many forms and leaves in many forms also. They die. They live. We must forget them and build.

This book speaks to the void that developed in me after discovering traitors in our midst. But it also speaks more forcefully to the strengths gained in discovering in our people a new critical judgement that will not just forgive and forget those that do us harm—regardless of who they are. We *all* must face the coming test and it will not be an easy one. But, most will not recognize that they are being tested and they will undoubtedly fail. The few who pass will start the re-building. They will begin the final movement for Kawaida (Afrikan Tradition and Reason), peoplehood and land. We continue to work and await them and leave with you this, the *Book of Life*.

Haki R. Madhubuti (Don L. Lee)
Poet-in-Residence
Howard University
8/28/73

*National Union for the Total Independence of Angola
**African Party for Independence of Guinea (Bissau) and Cape Verde Islands

WORLDVIEW

fact is stranger than fiction
here in america in the year of 1973
many black people don't even know how
we came to this land

some black people believe that
we were the first people
to fly
and that we came first class.

POSITIVE MOVEMENT WILL BE
DIFFICULT BUT NECESSARY

(for John O. Killens)

remember past ugly to memories of the *once*
to memories of the used to be
lost days of glory, the forgotten-forgiven history of the race:
when sun mattered and the night was for sleeping
and not for planning the
death of enemies.

beautiful
realpretty like morning vegetation
beautiful
like Afrikanwomen bathing in Tanzanian sun
beautiful a word now used exclusively to describe the
                    ungettable
            a word used to describe roaches disguised as
                    people that viciously misrule the world.
times is hard rufus & they gointa be harda
come on champ chop chop
hit hard   hit harda   catch up   chop chop
sleep less   eat right   rise earlier
whip dust into the eyes of excuse makers
talk to yr children about meaning,
talk to yr children about working for the race.
chop chop   hit hard   hit harda
beat it   beat it   beat it   now

in this world
we face our comings as hip slaves unknown to ourselves
unknown to the actual challenges of the race
do you know yr real name?
do you know the real reasons you are here?
check the smiles on yr enemies' faces
if you can identify yr enemies
they crawl from the earth in many faces: negroes,
militants, revolutionary integrationists, soul-brother
number 15, black capitalists, colored politicians

133

and pig-eaters lying about their diets.

listen now listen
open yr ears we got a number for you
listen, somebody is trying to tell us something,
listen, somebody is trying to pull our minds.
it ain't magic we be better if it will   listen
let the words seek greater levels of meaning
split in there   words be   beat it beat it words
beat it now
it ain't gypsy tales or trails
or false eyes frontin for the devil
it ain't about the happy ending of the west
unless you are reading the future wrong.

134

WE ARE SOME FUNNY "BLACK ARTISTS" AND EVERYBODY LAUGHS AT US

random house and double day publish the
"militant black writers"
who write real-bad about the
"money-hungry jew" and the "power-crazed irishman."
random house and double day will continue to publish the
"militant black writers"
while sending much of the profits received from the books
    by the
"militant black writers"
to Israel and Ireland to build a nation for the
"money-hungry jew" and the "power-crazed irishman"
while the
"militant black writers"
who write real-bad about white people
can't even get a current accounting of their
royalties from random house or double day
and black nation-building never crossed their minds.

135

RISE VISION COMIN
MAY 27, 1972

(for Osagyefo Kwame Nkrumah 1909-1972)

there is quietness   hear
time to regroup   time to rethink   time to reassess
the world we think belongs to somebody else.

there is quietness   hear
time to create an Afrikan-mind
time to create an Afrikan-mind in a european setting   Chaka
(if we had called the blood Afrikan 4 years ago he wd a
   had his
whole family out for the kill lookin for a crazy negro, an
   unamerican,
a communist, a no nothin tree swingin jungle waker-er)   but

there is quietness   hear
shootin for the 21st century with 19th century weapons
while the whi-te boy is walkin on the moon
& negroes are runnin down to moonlounge on hot-pants
   night
we some BAD diamond wearers, you Bad brother:
badly taught
badly situated &
badly organized   but

there is a quietness   hear
time to re-educate   time to redirect our limits   super
time to stop being the *buts* in the undefined, unfinished
sentences of the flesh-eaters: he's a first class doctor *but*
he's colored, she's one of the best teachers ever *but* she's
negro, he's a fine worker *but* he's black.   but
there is quietness   hear

we are what we are
we are what we are not
we are what we are going to be

we are what we are
the reflection the image the backward word world of what
the substance of that we must become the positive side of
    comin
send roy wilkins to Afrika if he don't act AFRIKAN
think him have mo wisdom than the OAU
a real credit to his race: bad credit a piece of 15th century
science fiction talkin bout his momma as if she was
    the enemy
a for real beatin down negro unsure of the space he occupies
if he occupies any   him show not invisible   we see rat
    through him
feel his opposite a walkin back steppin X-rated movie with
blocked vision   but
we comin

we are what we are not
think him Gulf Oil, IBM or GM the way he talk about
    industrializing
Afrika
if they took the water faucet from him he'd die of
    water-freeze

think him Dow Chemical or the Pentagon the way he talk
    about arming
Afrika
but we goin a need mo than wine bottles, promises & ray
    gun dreamin

think him Harvard or MIT the way he talk about educating
Afrika couldn't even teach a day care center if it was already
    taught

we are what we are going to be
comin sam   comin willie   comin mable   comin jesus malinda
    pepper
now u different
comin rise risin comin   talkin about doin it yoself   hunh
about institutionalizing yr thoughts yr actions comin risin

to
claim the tradition & collective culture of your world
   comin *rise*
rise junebug   beat evil back into the cold Zimbabwe
expose the enemy FRELIMO u goin a do it Angola   rise
now u different blood   new   stronger
stronger than storm bigger betta betta than a bad footed
   negro
in fifty dollar shoes comin runnin call u swift call u fast fasta
fasta than stolen Bar-B-Q in a baptist meetin on last sunday
   comin
live the land the purity of the first humans is in you comin *rise*
dash-on flash dodgin skyscrapers vacant lots & evil highs
with a conscious feel for earth for land for yrself comin rise
transformin reborn renurtured in purpose in goodness in
   direction new
u dynamite Musi where did u arrive from Kikuyu
where u been hidin Rastafarian   which way SWAPO
what universe did u crash thru NewArk   call u speed speeda
make yr own gas create yr own energy dig an escape hatch
   into us rise
redirectin our focus callin ourselves AFRIKANS
callin ourselves AFRIKAN men & women callin ourselves
   builders of the
FIRST callin ourselves stylers of tomorrow: the shape to
   come shaper
comin 21st century fly golden antelope a black lion is u simba
and the world is still here still evolving even the devil can't
stop that   gave us the worse Enemy EVER: *aint never seen
   nothin like the europeans* lost they taste fo life-living. but
they can't stop higher vision   can't stop newrisin right talkin
good doin it gettin it done Afrikans can't stop organized
   builders of righteousness
pull the fight together Guinea-Bissau
we with u southern Sudan   fight on runnin wise Mozambique
jump quick lightin FROLIZI   teach Nyerere   watch our backs
   Osagyefo
   guide our future Lumumba   describe our enemies Garvey
   we're comin Toure comin PAIGC goin to surprise the world

surprise
our father's Malcolm   we have mo than mouth mo than fast-
    talk
mo than Harvard rhetoric   we are comin

we are what we are
we are what we are not
we are what we are going to be
comin comin risin risin to a higher beat of Afrikan movement
    comin fast
dancin hard makin sense remembering Sharpeville
    remembering Orangeburg
comin remembering yesterday's plant risin out of the earth
    fast
challenging new thoughts challenging concepts of false gods
    comin *rise*
elevator up juju blackworld vibrations beatin us into eachother
    rise comin risin thru visions of Afrikanlove   rise   comin feet
get back negative   we comin shine   fightin thru spacesun
    son is
slidin closer to the expected comin nationalists
comin christians comin muslims comin pan-afrikanists ancient
    black spirits
    comin comin
rise buba rise brothers rise sisters rise people of the summer
    comin
comin comin come in come in come in
we are here quick

gathered gathered gathered

to save the future for our children.

HOOKED

the only time
the brother is sober is
when he tryin to
find another
high.

AFRIKAN MEN

(for Hoyt W. Fuller & Lerone Bennett, Jr.)

there is a certain steel-ness about you
the way u set the vision & keep it
the way u view the world & warn us.
the coming tomorrows the limited memory of what was
the image the reflection the realness of what is to be.

our pace is faster but without wisdom
our "advances" are louder yet without movement
our mistakes are many & often deadly
yet we seek examples seek the quality of substance
while the lies drop around us
making the actors into the reactors
and even though we don't wear for sale signs
we've been bought rather cheaply, yet

we
with the limited memories have learned
not to trust the easy music
not to trust the processed food
not to trust the comfortable compromise,
have learned
that love will not stop the enemies of the world
their nature will not allow them
to submit to the beautiful
& our minds quicken knowing that
if a rat is chewing at yr baby's skull
you don't negotiate you
kill it.

there is a certain stillness about you
unwilling to be pushed by the opportunities of the world,
your insight into the holocaust will not permit
fastness, non-movement or mistakes
you understand that these are the luxuries of the young
& the young have limited memories.

141

we've now passed the dangers of youth because
there is a certain steel-ness about you
the way u set the vision & keep it
the way u view the world & warn us.

SPIRIT FLIGHT INTO THE COMING

(For Amilcar Cabral (1925-1973), Imamu Amiri Baraka
and Congress of Afrikan People)

Ever get tired of people playing with yr life, playing with
yr children's lives, playing with blackness, playing with Afrika?
Ever get tired of other people telling you what you shd be
doing for yr self? Ever get tired of people posturing,
posing and profiling?
We all know niggers look good   but
We don't own nothing
We don't have no land
We don't have no army
We don't control no major institutions
We don't
We don't even teach our children how to be themselves
We don't influence black domestic policy
We don't influence foreign policy toward Afrika
We are a powerless, defenseless people   but we're
looking good, looking very good   step now   step
step now yo step now get in step brother   lookin very good
The white boy make the clothes and put em on the store
          dummy
and we, lookin good—out dress the dummy
Hey   step now   get in step brother   let's get a strong
line lookin good   step on in
We are a powerless, defenseless people   lookin very good
and don't even make the make-up we whiten our faces with
we don't do nothin except talk about what others need to be
doing for ourselves, while ourselves are too busy being
like others we talk about we don't want to be like
as ourselves wear their clothes better than they do, drive their
cars faster than they do, talk their language as well as they
    do
while it all spells out to be theirs as ourselves illusionize
about doin our thang and don't understand the world our
    selves
live in but ourselves are down there just below
nixon's toilet eatin pig meat and lying to our

children about blackness.
Witness the negro asst. asst. to the president's asst.
going thru his post black period talkin about what
the administration is doing for the race   maybe
him talkin about the Indianapolis 500.

We sick because we don't know *who we are*.
We sick because we don't have a *purpose* in life.
We sick because we don't have *direction* for ourselves.

Step in CAP: Congress of Afrikan People   step in
refix the world clear the rust from our eyes
navigate the wind, expose the enemy, inform the mind
connect the black organs. Work a wonder:
make the negro black and Afrikan again—even if
we don't wanta be. We don't wanta be here, but we are!

Everything else is Jive! negro congressmen
can't even pass a bill to save they people. Colored general
too busy welcoming home war criminals, probably kill his
    momma
for another star   star him in a John Wayne movie
one eyed negro Jewish dancer sleeping in the white house
hope him sleep there forever
dance sammy dance, dance sammy dance,
as our people gaze blankly at garbage men passing thru our
    communities
at midnight while
negro pimps fight their people for recognition from Agnew's
    momma.

Reflect the image CAP—step in somebody
shine brightness for a dead people.
show us that there is value in ourselves
prove to us that we are worth saving—heal the forgotten mind
the forgotten bodies of the east.
prove to us that we are worth saving
cure the negativism in us
provide the example   teach the doctrine

display identity:	we were builders of the first.
display purpose:	our children, our parents, our ancestors *great as we be*
display direction:	sharing land, raising our children, building a world the way a world is supposed to be built.

Everything else is Jive: Ph.D.'s in french, can't eat no french
can't farm no land with french. wake up showboat, wakeup
   showboat
Dr. Clearhead Knowitall Ph.D., summa cum laude U of
   Chicago 1973
now teaching the *psychology of blackness* in the suburbs
proving to the enemy—that taught him—how smart him is
what have you done for your people lately Dr. Knowitall?
what have you done for the race except, race away
waving flags about it's a human and class problem
ask your great, great, great grandmomma, fool,
was she raped from a continent due to the human/class
   problem?

Step in Imamu:
plant the seed and regulate the growth you are the
vegetation of life. bloods are getting up earlier now
catching the sun on the second mile run   getting ready
for the day's work getting ready for the heavy load
cleaning up. washing down. disciplining ourselves consistent
with nature now. getting ready to re-make the life in us,
telling ourselves how we back stepped into what we
now be. tomorrow is our coming.

Everything else is Jive: we got negroes arguing the necessity
   of Marx and Engels to empty-bellied children,
we got negroes married to white people speaking for the race.
don't no Arabs speak for Jews.
we slaves because we wanta be. we slaves because we
   wanta be.
unbelievable
but being a slave is hip

being a slave in america is *really* hip
slaves think they can buy their freedom
slaves drive big cars
slaves take dope
slaves love big houses
slaves teach blackness at big universities
slaves love their enemy
slaves love death in any form
slaves love paper money
slaves live for pleasure only
if we slaves be let free we'd buy ourselves back into slavery.
it is hip being a slave in America cause we got everything
    slaves need,
we're the richest slaves in the world.

Step in Imamu
all that is good and accomplished in the world takes work
work is what we need an abundance of
work for a better value system   work
work for ourselves like we work for general motors,
like we work for integration, like we work for the
son of mary   work
teach one   reach one   work and study
study the math, the physics, the chemistry   that is
    revolutionary
study the science of building   that is revolutuionary
study the inner workings of yr self   that is revolutuionary
think about building a livable world   that's revolutionary
meditate on a new way of life   that's revolutionary
Juba Juba Juba du
move Juba into agriculture like we move in fashions
work Juba work Juba work
Juba Juba Juba du now work Juba
write some work songs Juba work
paint some work pictures Juba work
play some work music Juba work
Juba Juba Juba du
work raw honey for the brain
work exercise for the dead blood cells

work life serum for the tired muscles
work chakula for the body
work the land into food
work to keep yr woman by yr side
work the evil into good
work the enemy into submission
work and organize organize and work
work and develop develop the work
work and study   study the work
work energizes Afrika and Afrikan people
work energizes Afrika and Afrikan people
All that is good and accomplished in the world takes work
Everything else is Jive

17 juni 1973

LIFE POEMS

1.
the best way to
effectively fight an
alien culture
is to live your own.

2.
pride in one's people is desirable
pride in black people is necessary for black people
but
pride must be properly cultivated
and displayed in moderation
too much pride alienates brother from brother
        alienates sister from sister
alienates us from community and nation
too little pride
confuses the natural direction we must take
and hinders the building of nations
pride in abundance is bad
too little pride is bad
strike a balance.

3.
is a sign of life in your face?
is the sign of life in your thoughts?
is the sign of life in your actions?
if not   there can be no life in you.
if so   you are life.

4.
there is life in men
men are life   but
when men put themselves above others
life becomes disproportionate and loses clarity
when a man puts material and worldly goods above humanity
our understanding of and value for real life ceases
his wife becomes something he sleeps with
his children become objects to order about
his friends become competition
the land becomes property to fence in
his aim in life is toward making it and getting over
his tradition ceases to have meaning
and is not passed on to his children
his tomorrows are now measured in material production &
        acquisition
and his future is that which he puts in the bank today.

5.
those who know
both ways
and proceed to take the incorrect one
may not be able to reverse themselves later.

6.
to know is to be
to be and not know is not to be
to know and not know that you know is not to know
to know and not be is not to know
to know is to be

7.
to seek all the answers of life
into yourself is to misunderstand life.
we are only a minute portion of all
that makes up life and our relationship
to other forms of life gives meaning to
our life.
we are all in the cycle of return and give.
understand yourself first but also go
outside of yourself so as to understand the
cycle of life.
seek answers of the world in the world
while understanding that the world
is part of you.

8.
it is true that nature   in time
will solve the world's problems
and resolve the world's disputes
however, nature and time are unpredictable
and may not act in our lifetime.
our understanding of life
demands that we respect nature & time
but our children's future
demands that we help nature solve our problems today
with the little time we have on earth.

9.
if we are not for ourselves
who is for us?
if we are men and women
why are other people giving us orders?

10.
there is much to be learned
there is much to be unlearned
to do both
takes an open mind and a mind that questions.
we can get correct answers   only
if we ask the correct questions.

11.
we have people in our midst
who can quote
every body from *can* to *can't*
but do nothing else.
theory without practice is like
a car without gas   is like
land without cultivation   is like
poetry without content.
men and women *act*
others re-act and talk about acting.
which are we?

12.
there are those
who have never left
home
but understand the universe.

13.
those who think nothing of themselves
are not full and cannot appreciate others
because they cannot appreciate themselves.
those who think only of themselves
have no room for others
and cannot appreciate others.
those who are secure in themselves
will not fear security in others
and
will be motivated toward the most secure of relationships
that of friendship
and friendship reinforces security.

14.
weak people
hide behind titles
and status to aid their egos.
weak people
attack from the rear.
watch your back
as you move forward.

15.
know yourself first
that which is good
that which is bad
correctly assess yourself
and you will not mistakenly assess your neighbors.

152

16.
we are not a tribe
we are a nation.
we are not wandering groups
we are a people.
we are not without land
there is Afrika.
if we let others define us
our existence, our definition will be dependent upon
the eyes, ears, and minds of others.
other people's definitions of us cannot be accurate for us
because their hurt is not our hurt,
their laughter is not our laughter,
their view of the world is not our view of the world.
other's definition of the world
is necessary for their survival and control of the world
and for us to adopt their view of the world is a necessary
step toward their continued control over us
therefore to let others define us is to assure
we *will* be a tribe,
we *will* be wandering groups,
we *will* be
landless
self-definition is the first step toward
self-control.

17.
if you know who you are
the identity of others
will be respected, appreciated
understood.

153

18.
talk little and listen with care
those who talk much
cannot hear the silences around them
cannot hear the noises around them
they hear only their own voice
and will mainly talk of themselves.
talk little and listen with care
there is more to the world than your own voice.

19.
if you are silent
no one can hear you coming
if you make much noise
your enemies can prepare for you.

20.
knowledge of self starts at home
understand that which is
closest to you first.
understanding that which is nearest
brings meaning to that
which is far.

21.
many people fear knowledge
knowledge stimulates change and most people fear change
to acquire knowledge is to grow
to grow is to change
growth without knowledge is not growth
growth with knowledge leads toward wisdom
there are few wise people in our time
and change is what we need

22.
if the people
think that they can buy everything or
that everything is for sale
then there is little left in life of real value.
they will spend their days making money
spend their evenings thinking about what to buy
and spend their weekends buying.
this is not normal and is in conflict with
the natural way of life,
if a people feel that they can buy everything
their values are corrupt and they too
can be bought and are not to be trusted.

23.
the need of expensive clothes, cars and homes
to impress others and yourself
only means
that you have no meaning without them
which also means
that you have no meaning with them.

24.
to
betray a trust
is to
cut yourself off from being
trusted.

25.
to be ignorant of the world around you
is slavery
to not want to know of the world around you
is death.

26.
we must be able to function within ourselves
we must build and develop our inner spirit and force.
this gives autonomy to our outer movements
as we seek to forcefully interact with the larger world.
if this interaction is to be successful
it must be a force with spirit behind it that
no one will doubt. such a spirit
and force can only come from a people who
have faith in themselves and the path they
have chosen for themselves.
we are an Afrikan people.

27.
to know nothing is a statement of negative being
to know nothing speaks to a condition of uselessness
to know nothing puts one at the mercy
of those who know.

28.
if you are confused
you'll bring confusion to
everything you touch.

29.
people who eat
everything that is placed before them
by anybody, anywhere
cannot be healthy
choose your food as you choose friends
with care and knowledge of its ultimate value.

30.
to go without food
brings an understanding
of the people who are foodless
but
to go without food
and know that none is forthcoming
brings an appreciation and understanding
of food and the foodless
that is unlearnable any other way.

31.
those who eat and need
many meals in a day
can not be eating the food that gives and maintains life.
life-giving foods such as vegetables and fruits
are the basis for good health and long life
and should be consumed modestly.
processed food from processed sources
produce a processed body with a processed mind;
produce men and women whose first love is to eat
and only aim in life is to
make it to the next meal.

32.
many of the modern day diseases
that hurt us did not exist many years ago.
however many years ago our diets didn't consist of:
powdered this and instant that,
frozen now and eaten later,
canned everything and contaminated water,
pour and mix and open and stir   all
preceded by any flesh of the world,
from fried monkey to boiled pig bellies,
you cannot sustain life with "foods"
out of boxes, cans, plastic and resealable jars.
you need live food for live bodies.
stay close to the earth
consume that which the earth naturally gives us.

33.
there is meaning here
in us under the weight of hours today
under the weight of misunderstanding of their world.
we clench our teeth, lie to our children and make it.
but the feared breaks through
the air is dirty and kills much,
the streets are trafficful and nothing moves,
the water is impure and slowly damages the drinker.
life cannot endure this way.
there is meaning here
if we seek it.

34.
the family is the basic unit of all nations.
the family structure has endured since recorded history
the family structure will continue to survive the sickness
of the day:
let the singles come,
let the bi-sexuals come,
let the homosexuals come,
let the non-family advocates come,
let the extreme individualists come,
let the unisexuals come,
let the transvestites come.
those are brief aberrations of a sick nation
and if the nation is to live and prosper
the family will live and endure because
the nation is families united.

35.
there is much special
about black women,
the way they endure,
the way they grow,
the way they build,
the way they love,
it is traditionally thought that black women
are the reflection of black men.
and black men the reflection of black women.

36.
only fools limit women.
the full potential of a nation
cannot be realized unless the
full potential of its women
is realized.
only fools limit women.

37.
a nation cannot grow without its women
the intelligence of a nation
is reflected in its women
who bear the children for the nation
and are charged with the early education of the nation.
a nation cannot have intelligent women
unless the women are treated intelligently
and given much love.

38.
the substance and mental attitude of a nation
can be seen in its women, in the way they act
and move throughout the nation being productive.
if the women have nothing to do it reflects
what the nation is not doing.
if the women have substance and responsible positions
the nation has substance and is responsible.

39.
if a woman covers herself with paints
of blues, reds, grays and yellows
she unknowingly kills her skin,
she unknowingly smothers life from the first layer covering.
to paint a flower white that is naturally red is to
close its breathing pores and interrupt its natural skin growth
the flower will soon die.
to paint black skin green, orange and other colors
is to display black skin as something that
should be hidden from the actual world
and slowly suffocated from life.

40.
it is normal
for man to look at woman
but
it is abnormal to look
at woman the way we
have been taught to
look at her in the western world.

41.
we have been given
only one standard of beauty which
is the exact opposite of our own self-image.
due to this we see beauty in others
and fail to see it in ourselves.
this leads to destructive self-concepts that
will not only affect our relationship
with ourselves but will affect our
relationship with the world for the worst.

42.
nothing is created
without a mind
that is creative.

43.
institutions that reflect and guide a people
are important and necessary.
nations are made up of people who
create institutions that give substance
to the nation and its people.
where are the black institutions that
give substance to black people?
most of us would have difficulty identifying
more than one of them.
we must have new institutions in order
to institutionalize new thoughts and actions.
we must make current black institutions more
accountable to the needs of black people whom they
say they serve.

44.
we sit in our used cars
talking bad about others who don't own used cars and
we think that we are better off.
wonder who is running the world
while we talk about used cars?

45.
if you are silent
few will know
your ignorance.

46.
we must work to make life,
we must study to understand life,
we must create in order to support & stimulate life,
we must build to maintain life.

47.
the more complex life becomes
the more confused are the people.
we live in a world where we
pay to be born,
pay to live and
pay to die.
when the people seek work
they are computerized and given numbers,
when the people speak of hunger
they are photographed and made to feel less than people,
when the people seek medical care
they are filed into lines and experimented with,
when the people ask for education
they are scorned and laughed at,
when the people seek truth to be truth
they are lied to and ridiculed.
for those who need to know
you mistake the people's smiles for thank yous
and their sincerity for stupidity.
the people are not so soft and naive
as not to be able to remove complexity
and wipe out confusion
when they bring the hour.

48.
you do not save people
by putting water on their foreheads
or by immersing them in the deep.
save people
by being and by telling them the truth.

49.
beware of quick smiles
and fast words.
one who smiles overmuch
mis-uses the face.
one who talks too fast
seldom says anything worth listening to.
quick smiles and fast words
fool the weak,
confuse the strong,
do damage to the face   and
mis-use the language.

50.
best teachers
seldom teach
they be and do.

51.
you
are nothing
as long as
nothing is on your
mind.

52.
let us not seek to impress our people
with the eloquence of our words.
words cannot feed the hungry,
words cannot clothe or house the needy,
words cannot heal the sick,
words cannot plant the food.
words take us away from the doing.
speak carefully and with substance
and
you will not have to speak much about nothing
if this is done
your presence will be welcomed,
the people will speak highly of you at family gatherings
and you will be sought after by many.

53.
how many of our children
have seen the ocean's ripple
or have felt the morning wetness
of country
vegetation
or picked the just ripened fruit from trees or vines
or enjoyed the afternoon sun bathing
their bodies as they played in the green.
there is little that is green in the cities
other than the broken stop lights and
artificial grass.
our children's dreams are lost among the
concrete of too many promises
waiting for elevators to take them
to the top floors of public housing.

54.
corruption comes because we disrupt
and confuse the meaning of life.
we reorder natural and human
values to those of:
making money,
gaining power,
searching for sex,
pursuing fame,
seeking status
and lying to our children about life.
we need a new system of values speaking
to the real meaning of humanity.
corruption breeds corruption
the non-corrupt cannot live among
the corrupt and not become corrupt also,
one either leaves and exposes
or one becomes corrupt
there is no compromise,
there is no in between.

55.
when you work for yourself
you must *work* for yourself.
either we use the time we have wisely
or we do not use our time wisely.
if we say that our day starts at 6:30 a.m.
then it must. if we start at 7:30 a.m.
we are already an hour behind   an hour that
cannot be made up.
our enemies work 24 hours a day and
do not have hours to make up.
there
is no substitute for work.
but
there is a substitute for talking about work.

work!

56.
we do not equate
poverty with blackness
nor do we equate the lavish
use of wealth with blackness.
we now live in a time
where the many go without
while for the few we have entrusted to lead us
luxuries have become needs.

57.
the cities kill the will,
dull the senses,
make white the eyes and
stop the future in us
before it starts.
if we survive the west
we survive the worst,
but let us not become
worse in our survival.

58.
a people without their culture
are a people without meaning.
a people without their culture
are a people without substance.
a people without their culture
are a people without identity, purpose and direction.
a people without their culture
are a dead people.

59.
the old of our people
are the elders of the race
and must be listened to,
must be looked after,
must be given meaningful work,
must be loved and cared for,
must be treated with the highest respect.
the elders of the race
are the reason we are here.

60.
to hate one's self and one's people
is not normal
to perpetually wish to be like other people
is not normal
to act against one's self and one's community
is not normal
that which is normal for us
will never be normal for us
as long as the abnormal   defines what
normality is.

167

61.
we now have in our midst
people who *only* read and write and talk or argue.
they play with concepts and ideas,
can quote you the theory of the world,
can discourse for days on the meaning of life,
have usually an answer for everything and if they don't
have the answer they consult each other until
they come up with an answer.
they are powerless,
they are defenseless,
they have no land and mainly live in the cities.
they do not control major institutions
they do not control production,
they do not control distribution,
they do not make decisions on major policy for the nation,
they do not control the armed forces.
they would starve to death if somebody else
didn't bring them their food.
these are defenseless and powerless people.
they play with concepts and ideas and
divorce themselves from implementation.
they are not to be feared, they are to be re-educated.

62.
a man becomes the best runner in the country
because that is what he has been taught to be
and he wishes it and works hard for it.
a woman becomes the best doctor in the country
because that is what she has been taught to be
and she wishes it and works hard for it.
a man becomes the best hustler in the country
because that is what he has been taught to be
and he wishes it and works hard for it.
the major reason we don't work for our people
like we work at being runners, doctors and hustlers
is because no one has taught us to be and act as a people
or what the value and importance of being a people means.
therefore, we are busy being the best runners, doctors,
and hustlers in the country.

63.
our belief in our people
can only be measured by the
belief we have in ourselves
if we do not believe in ourselves
our belief in our people will not be real
because   we are the people.

64.
afrikan holidays
are holy days:
teach the history,
legitimize the nation,
reinforce the traditions
and
reunite the families.

65.
look beyond tomorrow
it will help you
accomplish that which is needed
today.

66.
a son needs direction if he is to be strong & work for the race
he does not need harsh words
about the way he should be
or words about how he should do this or that.
Fathers
study your own ways
so that your actions may guide him past the pitfalls of life
the best teacher is you being the example
of what others talk about.

67.
don't talk about
organizing the city or the world for self-reliance
when you can't organize
your own house or community.
start with self
and move to those closest to you
and each in turn do the same.
it is a slow but effective process
and it is better to be
slow and effective than to be
fast, ineffective and seen in all parts
of the city talking
nonsense.

68.
we know more about
how to kill than we know about
how to save.
our medicine is curative rather than preventive.
the weapons of war are more numerous
than schools, hospitals or places of worship.
we destroy small nations to save them from ideology.
we teach our children the ways of life
as we act out the ways of destruction.
our contradictions are catching up with us
and we will fall very fast in our lies and acts
because we are ill-prepared for saving.
we know more about how to kill.

69.
nations are like people
they need each other
no nation is truly independent
all nations are interdependent
however some nations are more dependent
on other nations than on themselves
so as
to put them at the mercy of other nations.
strengthen yourself internally before you seek
strength from the outside.

70.
the need to impress the world
shows little understanding of the world.
the need to make good impressions
means you have false impressions
the need to be The Best
is to misunderstand what best is.
the major reason for competition
is to take us away from cooperation and collective actions
and allows the many to be subtly controlled by the few.
put faith in the ability of each other
while strengthening the weaknesses of each other.
this is the natural order of things
and you will stand out
like vegetation in the desert
and will attract much water.

71.
it is said that,
"death is no threat to a people
who are not afraid to die."
yet
life today in part is controlled
by those who are afraid
to live.
a reordering of the world is due.

72.
there are no vacations
when a people are enslaved
there are just more sophisticated
forms of slavery disguised as
three weeks off with pay.

73.
understand the enemy within
and
the enemy without
will
be easier to deal with.

74.
we love our dogs
more than we love ourselves.
we feed our dogs three times a day.
we clothe our dogs in dog clothes.
we walk and talk with our dogs every day.
we call our dogs "man's best friend."
we play with our dogs and buy them dog toys.
when our dogs get sick we see that they get the
best of care.
if we dealt with each other one fourth as well
as we deal with our dogs this would be
more of a people world than a world
livable for dogs.

75.
if i make mistakes
tell me about them while i live
don't wait until i have left the earth
and then accuse me of contradictions
i may not have been aware of.

76.
in seeking answers
don't go too far on too little
you may not make it back

77.
black people
are all musicians
even though
they don't all
play instruments.

78.
move around wishes
and begin to control reality.
you can't wish good life upon a people,
you can't wish the best education upon a people,
you can't wish shelter and clothing upon a people,
you can't wish self determination upon a people,
you can't wish self respect upon a people.
you can't wish self defense upon a people.
replace most of your wishes with work
and you will not have time to wish often
you'll be too busy harvesting your crop.

79.
knowledge is like water
it is nourishment for those who seek it
and wasted on those who misuse it
but for all whom it touches
it does some good   so like water
let's spread knowledge worldwide.

80.
if you need to learn nuclear physics
you go to a nuclear physicist.
if you need to know how to work the land
you go to a farmer.
if you need to know how to build a house
you go to a carpenter.
if you need to know mathematics
you go to a mathematician.
if you need to know medicine
you go to medical school.
when all is learned that is needed to be learned
you return to your people and set up your own
schools for your own people.
this is one way
to fight and win wars.

81.

your world is in your eyes.
if you believe you have a future it will be in your eyes.
if you are well physically and mentally
it will be seen in your eyes.
if one is good and is to be trusted look into their eyes.
if one is evil their eyes will not hide it.
if one is afraid, their fear will look at you.
if one has strength, the part of the body
to show it first will be the eyes.
with the eyes you cannot deceive
nor can you make them up as to hide
their real meaning.
most people will not look you directly
in the eye.
some hide behind sunglasses,
some hide behind just not looking at you.
the eyes tell too much.
if you seek answers
do not look at one's possessions or non-possessions
to tell the way of a person
look into their eyes.

82.

why do most of our leaders who
start out as a part of their people
and genuinely work for their people
end up
living away from their people and
telling their people what *they* should
be doing while getting upset because
their people question their credibility?

83.

you can't define
tomorrow if you don't
know where you are
today.
if you do not read,
read!
if you do not think,
think!
add to reading and thinking
meditation.
meditate at a minimum of 1 hour a day
evenly divided.
1/2 at sunrise and 1/2 at sunset.
this will balance the internal
with the external and
bring knowledge of a *force*
greater than self.

84.

pimps and prostitutes
are the sickness of a nation.
are the sickness of a people.
but if a people are not able
to offer the pimp and prostitute
a tomorrow or a future that is believable
the sickness will remain
and worsen
until the death sets in.

85.
few things of value in life
are accomplished individually.
nations are built collectively,
schools are built collectively,
farms are farmed collectively,
holidays are observed collectively,
this is natural for those who have
direction and respect each other.
those who work share in the
goods produced and profits made.
those who are unable to work
are taken care of.
when the people of a nation begin
to use "I" more than "we"
the nation is dispersed and is in trouble.

86.
a negative act is a lesson,
a contradiction can be learned from and
there is meaning in evil
for those who are seeking good.

87.
if one
can be bought for $50.00
they can be bought twice for $100.00
if one will sell their self to you
they will sell their self to others, also.

88.
we wound each other
with false words,
evil eyes,
often lies
and pettiness disguised as criticism.
watch those who are closest to you
some of them carry the knives
that cut the deepest as they
agree with you while you die bleeding.
yet still,
even among the closest of enemies
the best defense
for your position
is your practicing
it.

89.
how many of us can
run a mile without tiring,
touch our toes without
bending our knees,
do pushups and pullups
without damaging our bodies for life?
the body needs exercise
just as the mind needs exercise,
the mind cannot function at its
peak unless the body is physically
at its peak.
reading, studying and doing practical research and work
develops the mind.
morning exercise, physical work
and practical eating
develop the body
the mind and the body   must work as one,
for you to be one.

90.
your name
tells us who you are,
where you come from,
where you are going,
how you may get there
and who is going with you.
your name
is legitimization of the past
confirmation of the present
and direction for the future.

91.
people play with the spirit
and at being "spiritual."
they cut themselves off from the real world
while meditating on rocks and water
and turning the sun into the moon.
the reality of life is confused abstractions
and the people do not understand them
and dismiss them as being crazy.
the people are correct.
meditation is needed and necessary
but must move the higher levels of the mind
into the people and not away from the people.
we meditate to maintain a balance in ourselves
while seeking greater wisdom of the outside.
it is not wise to seem abstract
when that which is practical is needed.
the most spiritual of acts
is
how positively you relate to and
work with your people.

178

YOU WILL RECOGNIZE YOUR BROTHERS

You will recognize your brothers
by the way they act and move throughout the world.
there will be a strange force about them,
there will be unspoken answers in them.
this will be obvious not only to you but to many.
the confidence they have in themselves and in
their people will be evident in their quiet saneness.
the way they relate to women will be
clean, complimentary, responsible, with honesty and as
partners.
the way they relate to children will be
strong and soft full of positive direction and as example.
the way they relate to men
will be that of questioning our position in this world,
will be one of planning for movement and change,
will be one of working for their people,
will be one of gaining and maintaining trust within the culture.

these men at first will seem strange and unusual but
this will not be the case for long.
they will train others and the discipline they display
will be a way of life for many.
they know that this is difficult
but this is the life that they have chosen
for themselves, for us, for life:
they will be the examples,
they will be the answers, they will be the first line builders,
they will be the creators,
they will be the first to give up the weakening pleasures,
they will be the first to share a black value system,
they will be the workers,
they will be the scholars,
they will be the providers,
they will be the historians,
they will be the doctors, lawyers, farmers, priests
and all that is needed for development and growth.
you will recognize these brothers
and
they will not betray you.

Book of Life

7
Earthquakes and Sunrise Missions
(1984)

POETRY

Poetry will not stop or delay wars, will not erase rape
  from the landscape,
will not cease murder or eliminate poverty, hunger or
excruciating fear. Poems do not command armies, run
school systems or manage money. Poetry is not
intimately involved in the education of psychologists,
physicians or smiling politicians.

in this universe
the magic   the beauty   the willful art of explaining
the world & you;
the timeless   the unread   the unstoppable fixation
with language & ideas;
the visionary   the satisfiable equalizer screaming for
the vitality of dreams   interrupting false calm
demanding fairness and a new   new world are the
poets and their poems.

183

Poetry is the wellspring of tradition, the bleeding
connector to yesterdays and the free passport to
  futures.
Poems bind people to language, link generations to
each other and introduce cultures to cultures.
Poetry, if given the eye and ear, can bring memories,
issue in laughter, rain in beauty and cure ignorance.
Language in the context of the working poem can
raise the mindset of entire civilizations, speak to two
year olds and render some of us wise.

To be touched by living poetry can only make us
  better people.
The determined force of any age is the poem, old as
ideas and as lifegiving as active lovers. A part of any
answer is in the rhythm of the people; their heartbeat
comes urgently in two universal forms, music and
poetry.

for the reader   for the quiet seeker
for the many willing to sacrifice one syllable
mumblings and easy conclusions
poetry
can be that gigantic river
that allows one to recognize
in the circle of fire
the center of life.

184

The Petty Shell Game

with raped memories and clenched fists. with small
thoughts and needless time we indulge in destruction
bathing ourselves in comedy and fraudulent posture:
    willa mae is going with big daddy t and lula is
    pregnant and don't know who the father is,
    cleavon said that the father is "we the people."

quite a profound statement among losers and people
beaten into the gutter and like desperate rats continue
to destroy with:
    richard g. is a faggot and pretty johnny is bald
    under that rag on his head, rev. jones is going
    with sister mary & sister emma & sister sara
    &   but
the important issue here always, especially among the
  young is
where is the party this weekend &
where you get that boss smoke, man?
yet, as the hipped whipped often say, "only fools
work" not daring to take into consideration that
"fools" built the western world and raped the rest of
it. yes, "only fools work" as we non-fools every early
monday morn   fight each other for position outside
the state welfare department.

& if there is time
wait
measure stillness and quiet.
redo moments of kindness
& if there is misunderstanding
change yr words & come again.

We can do what we work to do.
slaves have children,
drive tanks,
visit playboy clubs, buy
$60 ashtrays and get extremely
angry at children leaning against their
cars.

186

Wait.
yes, there is time for love   but
equal & often more moments must be given to
war.
& even within this madness
special seriousness must be
got to be allocated for the
children

We can do what we work to do
measure stillness and quiet
noise is ever present.
if we are not careful we will not
hear the message
when it
arrlves.

EXPECTATIONS

people Black and stone
be careful of that which is designated beautiful
most of us have been taught from the basements
of other people's minds.
often we mistake strip mining for farming
and that that truly glows is swept under
the rug of group production.
it is accepted in america that beauty is
thin, long & the color of bubble gum.
few articles generated by the millions are beautiful
except   people.

trust people
one by one
the darker they come
the more you can give your heart,
their experiences most likely are yours
or will be yours.
even within the hue & hueless
among them are those
who have recently lost their
ability to recall.

they can hurt you
drop you to your knees with words
much of that which blasts from their mouths
is not them   the offense is
they do not know that it is not them
as they rip your heart open
and reduce you to the
enemy.

THE WRITER

in america the major reward for
originality
in words, songs and visual melody
is to have dull people
call you weird
while asking what
you do for a living.

EVERYTHING'S COOL:
BLACK AMERICA IN THE EARLY EIGHTIES

in middle, rural, urban & combative america
it is a laborious challenge to explain racism and
  oppression
to a people that have among their members a
materially comfortable leadership and a complacent &
ignorant middle class that eats regularly, wears de-
signer socks, ventures into debt at will, loses them-
selves in artificial stimuli, are extraordinarily mobile &
largely expect the serious rewards of life in the next
world.

freedom is often confused with owning cars & bars
and being able to cross state lines without passports.
functional knowledge (e.g., computer technology,
producing food, governing self) is measured in one's
ability to quote the evening news & pontificate for
days on the merits of astrology or star power as it
relates to Black struggle. to many the haitian crisis
is a new dance, el salvador is mexican food, south
afrikan apartheid is a media creation and the only
foreign policy that is crucial to their lives is the paris
contribution to the yearly *ebony* fashion fair.
liberation on the real side is possessing the capacity
to swim in self pleasure & mundane acquisitions
without negative comment or challenge.

this cool crowd
believes that the majority of Black people suffer
because they are either lazy, unskilled, not motivated
or unlucky and that color & previous condition of
slavery is not germane to their current living status.
to quietly suggest to them that most of our people
exist in a state of dispirited boredom & wrecking
poverty only confirms their "lazy or unlucky" theory &
is accepted as a comment on the deficiencies of the
Black poor & have little to do with other people

and their economic & political systems. this
mindset is wide spread among all cultures in america
& for poets or anyone non-white to issue reminders
is considered rude and "sixtyish" & is to be
construed as a note on one's own inability to "make
it" in the mainstream of the melted dreams.

the conscientious doer is labeled disrupter & is
perceived as an economic failure (the only kind that
counts) and one's words fall on blown out ears
& pac-man mentalities. the prevailing beliefs in the
land encourage individuals, families, corporations
and police departments to pursue their most
outlandish desires; representing an understatement of
acute confusion, where cultural and traditional values
are lost to the latest fads & electronic games.
it is clear and crystal
that the one
undeniable freedom
that *all* agree exist
for Black people in america
is the freedom
to
self-destruct.

THE SECRETS OF THE VICTORS

(the only fair fight is the one that is won
—Anglo-Saxon Proverb)

forever define the enemy as less than garbage,
his women as whores & gutter scum,
their children as thieves & beggars,
the men as rapists, child molesters & cannibals,
their civilization as savage and
beautifully primitive.

as you confiscate the pagan's land, riches & women
curse them to your god for not being productive,
for not inventing barbed wire and DDT,
perpetually portray the *natives*
as innocent & simple-minded while eagerly
preparing to convert them to *your way*.

dispatch your merchants with
tins & sweets, rot gut & cheap wines.
dispatch your priest armed with
words of fear, conditional love and
fairy tales about strangers dying for you.
dispatch your military
to protect your new labor pool.

if there is resistance
or any show of defiance
act swiftly & ugly & memoriable.
when you kill a man
leave debilitating fear in the hearts of his
father, brothers, uncles, friends & unborn sons.
if doubt exists as to your determination
wipe the earth with his
women, girl children & all that's sacred;
drunken them in bodacious horror.
upon quiet, summon the ministers to
bless the guilty as you publicly
break their necks.

191

---

after their memories fade intensify the teaching.

instruct your holy men
to curse violence   while
proclaiming the Land Safe
introducing
the thousand year Reign of the Victors
as your Scholars
re-write the history.

IS TRUTH LIBERATING?

if it is truth that binds
why are there
so many lies   between
lovers?

if truth is liberating
why
are people told:
they look good when they don't
they are loved when they aren't
everything is fine when it ain't
glad you're back when you're not.

Black people in america
may not be made for the truth
we wrap our lives in disco
and sunday morning sermons
while
selling false dreams to our children.

lies
are refundable,
can be bought on our revolving
charge cards   as
we all catch truth
on the next go round
if
it doesn't hurt.

THE SHAPE OF THINGS TO COME

(December, 1980—what some people do to themselves is
only the first chapter in what they will do to others)

in naples, italy
the earth
quaked and three hundred thousand are
without beds, toilets and knowledge
of loved ones.
hourly revisions enlarge the dead & injured.
normal shortages exist adding
burial coverings
for the young
(evidently falling into the earth by the thousands is
not punishment enough)
the word goes out
to the makers and shapers of sordid destinies
that
"this is the time to make the money"
immediately
quicker than one can pronounce
free enterprise
like well-oiled rumors   or
elastic lawyers smelling money
plastic coffins appear
& are sold at dusk behind the vatican
on the white market.
in italy in the christian month of eighty
in the bottom of unimaginable catastrophe
the profit motive endures
as
children replenish the earth in
wretched abundance.

NEGRO LEADERSHIPS

our leaders are manufactured
in upstate new york in nobackbone field
just outside the catskills
on the yes plantation.
most are conceived with fools gold
in their teeth & jelly beans in their
thinking units & slide out of the incubator
  dancin doin the rump the charlie charlie bump
  the rump the knee bends the crawl but but up
their palms are greased with pig's oil &
automatically turn upward when near money.
they define their interest identical to that
of the major diamond & gold producers in the world.
negro leaderships share more than a need for greed
most have rusty knees, purple tongues & dry lips.
sport pot bellies, sore buttocks & manicured toenails
& excrete waste frontal.
  get it leroi step willie do the rump rump shuffle
  now tongue out eyes big spread yo butt now
they are trained at the best divinity schools,
do not spit verbs, read secular materials or
ponder too deeply about the negro problem.
black theology is blasphemous
& they view the world's enemy as
atheistic communism, scientific humanism &
thinking black women.

taught from birth 101 ways to say
no
to the realities of their people
the only value that
lights their fire
is
women bearing gifts,
an upward turn in the money market and
invitations from the mayor to march
in the annual st. patrick's day parade.

---

to see her is to realize why man was made different. is to realize why men were cut rough & unready & unfinished. the contrast would be like a magnet. and we fell into each other like wind with storm, like water into waiting earth. this woman black, this unbelievable wonder, would test the authenticity of a man's rough. a rap of beautifully rhymed words would not work with her. a well-rehearsed smile on the good side of your face or that special gleam from under your tanned shades could not penetrate this woman black. even the whole of you, in your pants tight with life, did not cause undo motion in her.

woman means more than woman
more than brown thighs
black lips, quick hips &
unfounded rumors

more than the common, more than the rational & irrational, more than music, more than rough stones & unread books, more than keepers of the kitchen, more than berry black, mellow yellow & town brown, more than quick pussy, more than european names followed by degrees, more than nine to five order takers, more than fine, more than fox evil eyes big legs tight hips or women of the summer.

this is why i write about you. i want to know you better. closer. so this is my message to you. not a study. not a judgement or verdict. just observations and experiences. a lifestory, specifically the last sixteen years. above all poems of *love* going against that which is mistakenly passed off as *love*. this is a collection of intense feeling and complete touch. these are poems that were not ripe or ready for earlier books. these are poems that had to come to you in their own time, their own color & meaning. i have tried to do you justice in all of my works, but this Woman of the Sun, is the real test of my seriousness & dedication to you. my mother & her mother are here. my father's mother is here. my sister is here. the women black that i have loved & loved & loved & still love are here.

my wife, quietly, as is her way, travels throughout these
pages. this is the work that i slept, ate and travelled with. this
is the beginning & middle the overtouched, with memories
from arkansas to michigan. this is an inadequate gift to the
other half of me, and to the whole of you. the you that often
goes unnoticed, unheard & unthanked. the you that is lost is
in the power plays of men and life.

woman black
i have tried to write about you
words
in a language strange & not of our making
words
refreshingly new
clean, lively, honest & uncomplicatedly indepth
words
forging & fighting their way into meaning
knowing too that
words
are like people are like you
woman black
& if left to simple interpretation
could be twisted, misused & misunderstood.
i will write about you with loving care
my woman
this is my pledge to you for already
there is too much confusion surrounding
someone as wordless as
you.

loved one this is a tribute to the beauty and strength of you, a
comment on the good & bad of you, a commitment to the
inside & out of you, a confession to the limited understanding
of you, an appreciating love note to the intricate you. lady love
sixteen years of you are here. over a decade of joy, struggle,
hurt & growth. you have brought meaning & purpose to my
life, have connected me to the tangibles & moved me beyond
the rhetoric of ideas to the necessity of deeds. this is my testi-
mony to you who have taught me & my comeback to those of

you i have failed. please know that i have tried & will continue to go
against *whatever* for & with you. finally, these poems; these words say as much about me as they do about you. there are no real spaces separating us. *we are one. believe it.* believe in it. women. *women of the sun.*

MATURITY

emma jean aged one night
back in september of '63
it was after them girls
had received death in alabama
on their knees
praying
to the same god,
in the same church,
in the same space,
she prayed.

she aged that night
after the day had gone
and left her with her thoughts.
left her with the
history of her people in
america.
emma jean matured that night
and knew that in a country
that killed the children
under
the eyes of *their* god   that
she nor her people
were safe.

emma jean
decided back in september of '63
that she would let her people
know that they were not safe in
america
this is what she has done
and is doing   if she has not found you
look for her   kiss & hug her
thank her and then help her
to help us
mature.

ABORTION

she,
walla (queen) anderson
miss booker t. washington jr. high of 1957,
miss chicago bar maid of 1961
had her first abortion at 32
after giving birth to
john (pee wee) jackson at 14,
mary smith at 15 and a half,
janice wilson at 17,
dion jones at 19,
sara jones at 21,
and
richard (cream) johnson at 27.

on a sun-filled day
during her 32nd year
after
as many years of aborting
weak men who would not stand
behind their own creations
she
walla (queen) anderson
by herself   alone   without consultation
went under the western butchers
to get her insides
out.

SAFISHA

1.
our joining into one proceeded like
sand through a needle's eye.
slow, bursting for enlargement & uncertainty.
a smoothing of passion and ideas
into spirited permanence and love.

there are decades of caring in you,
children loving that makes the father
in me active and responsible.
you forecasted the decline of marble shooting
& yo yo tricks, knowing too that hopscotch
& double dutch could retard early minds if
not balanced with challenges and language.

you are what brothers talk about
when serious & committed to loving life.
when examples are used to capture dreams
you are that woman.
for me you are summer at midlife,
daring spirit and middlenoon love
and the reason i return.

2.
dark women are music
some complicated well-worked
rhythms
others   simple melodies.
you are like soft piano
black keys dancing between
& not becoming the white.
you bring dance & vision into our lives.
it is good & good
to be your
man.

WINTERMAN

janice was winter
she had been made cold by
years of maltreatment rough years
of loneliness and false companionship
and now in the middle of her time
she refused to ever take another chance with a
blackman.

janice cursed the race. didn't see no good that black
people ever done. raised on a plantation where her father was
a sharecropper she watched her mother, in her twilight years,
steal away to jesus. the bible was more than solution, more
than heaven after earth, it was food and water. it was ideas and
values steeped in fear and peaceful salvation.

janice ran north at twenty and between her twenty-first and
twenty-seventh year visited every store front church on the
west and south sides of chicago. she now fashions herself a
true missionary of the living gospel. her mission was to save
black men from the evil ways. she wanted black men to be like
mr. golding, the husband of the white woman she did day work
for. mr. golding took care of his family, had a big house and ate
dinner with his family every night that he didn't have to work
late (he worked late at least twice-a-week).

most black men thought janice was fine but foolish. after loving
her many would brakelight fast. disappear, most leaving without
an explanation. it came out later that some of them didn't like
being preached at at the point of sexual climax. others felt that
she prayed too much and were uncomfortable with being com-
pared to judas. after as many men as churches janice in her
thirty-fifth year decided to close her legs and like her
mother give her life, completely and unshared, to the only man
in her life she declared had never failed her. jesus would now
be the only man in her heart. it is not known exactly when dur-
ing that year she was called but rumor has it that the *ultimate*

light touched her the day after billy william, her last lover, start-
ed seeing her best and only friend minnie lou turner.

janice cursed the race. didn't see no good in black people. she
turned slavishly and slowly toward her employers and began to
live in. arlington heights, illinois was clean, peaceful and few
black people lived there.

it was winter and windy
it was cold and white   and
jesus,
sweet, sweet jesus
was her man.

LOVEPOEMS

1.
lately
your words are drugged passages
with razor edges
that draw blood & tears
     and
memories of less difficult moments
when   love
that beautiful   overused   emotion-packed commitment
charged the body.
love
momentarily existed
actually transformed us
defying the odds
flourishing   enlarging us
if only for seconds
seconds that were urgently expected
and
overneeded.

2.
there are rumors afloat that love
is ill.
intimacy at best is overnight
clashes
and morning regrets.
are
bodies underwashed in strange bathrooms
as lovers
& others   bang the door
softly running.

steppin cautiously in cracked silence
to spread rumors   that
love
is a diseased bitch
deserving death and quick
cremation.

3.
do not wait to be loved
seek it,
the unexplainable.
fight for love
not knowing whether you have
lost or accomplished
poetic possibilities.
dig deep for love
search while acknowledging
the complexity of the heart & fading standards.
in seeking love use care.
to let strangers come into you
too quickly
may make you a stranger to yourself.

4.
from dawn to dusk in cities
that sunrises often fail to visit

we imprisoned light
& generated heat.

you are seedless grapes and
bright stars at winter & wind.
there are voices in your smiles
and confirmation in the parting of your lips.

THE CHANGING SEASONS OF IFE

she is quality and light
a face of carob and ivory
of broad smiles and eyes that work.
she dresses in purples
& touches of aquablue.
plants grow profusely in her earthpots.
she seeks standards,
will not accept questionable roses or tapped water.
her taste is antique and bountiful heritage,
her music often void of melody
is firetone and harsh truths.
it is known that
dark rhythms played in & out of her early years
leaving temporary scars that lined her future
as beauty has it
wine is shared with shadows on prolonged trips
her smile broad & brandy
makes small miracles
emerge.

LADY DAY

hearing from you are smiles in winter
you   as you are
you warm and illuminating spaces
bring
blooming fruit in ice age times
with heated heated voices

believe me when i say
men will listen to you
most
will try to please you

there will be sun & thunder & mudslides
in your life
you will satisfy your days with work & laughter
and sunday songs.
your nights like most nights will
conjure up memories of easier seasons
happier suntimes and coming years

earthcolors and rainbows will enter your heart
when least expected
often
in small enduring ways   like this
lovesong.

SOME OF THE WOMEN ARE BRAVE

her strength may have come from
not having the good things early in life
like
her own bed, unused clothes,
"good looks," uncritical friends
or
from the knee of her great grandmother.
whatever path she took
she was learning to become small danger.

organizer of mothers,
overseer of broken contracts,
a doer of large deeds,
unafraid of sky scrapers & monotone
bureaucrats.
monotones labeled her demands crippling & unusual.
she urged drinkable water, working elevators,
clean playgrounds, heat, garbage collection
and the consolation of tenant's dreams.

many damned her,
others thought her professional agitator & provocateur
dismissing her as a
man hating bulldagger
that was communist inspired.

she was quick burn against the enemy
a stand up boxer unattached to niceties
and the place of women.
she was waterfalls in the brain
her potency as it comes
needs to be packaged & overnight expressed
to Black homes; to be
served with morning meals.

SEARCH VOID OF FEAR

bronzed fire among the cold of cold,
she was happy moments & clear fields.
she was touch & yellow
softrose with eyes that begged of sleep,
eyes that penetrated the cold of cold.

g.c. was lover & giver
searcher void of fear.
distances would be her metaphor
from cleveland to afrika over ocean & desert
travel expressed the search in her,
highlighting the afrikan in her.

just around her 8th season
g.c. passed through devastating hurt,
resulting in early burial of her man.
this is not talked of. her ancestors
demanded that she not be imprisoned with
dead thoughts or warm memories.

she was destined to be
searcher void of fear and
cold seconds should not detour
a softrose with eyes that begged of sleep.
often
she was happy moments & clear fields,
she was sun-riped and ready for war
indeed
ready for love.

WOMENBLACK: WE BEGIN WITH YOU

(for Safisha)

our women we begin with you
black, beige, brown, yellowblack and
darkearth we dropped from your womb
in joyscreams lifegiver
you're worlds apart from the rest.

our women
imagine a warm breeze in any city
in the west that will not choke you,
be wife, be mother, a worker or professional
maker you still my lady.
our women
of fruits & vegetables
of greens & color   of sounds & pot holes
of mountains & earth clearing danger   from
doorways who did not ruin their teeth & bodies
with the blood of pigs & cattle or fried chicken
after stumppin at bob's place til five in the daylight.
partyin was almost like a job
in motion on the run we are the rhythm people.

womenblack
unusual maker you say,
fine as all getout you say,
finer than lemonade in the shade,
we are a part of you maker, woman of
the autumn earth mother of sunlight
& i seldom say "i love you"
love is not our word. love belongs to
soap operas & comic books, is the true
confessions of the pale people from
the winter's cold.
we are the people of motion, move on motion
dance on, summer, summer lady.

womenblack we care about you
a deep & uncontrollable penetrative
care   as we listen to our own hearts,
whatever the weather.
you don't have to build a pyramid
in order to be one & you are still my
maker rhythm, rhythm lady.

our women we begin with you
black, beige, brown, yellowblack and
darkearth we dropped from your womb
in joyscreams lifegiver
you're worlds apart from the best.
you are in me & i in you
deep
deep and endless
forever
touch to touch,
end to beginning
until the stars kiss the earth
and
our music will be songs of liberation.

STRUGGLE

some called her
sunshine others berryblack
she was woman twice
laid way way back
her smile was winning-wide
her teeth glowed and captured light
she was woman twice
men thought her mighty nice

deep black off brown and mississippi grown lula mae was
careful. she had experienced the heartaches, heard the sto-
ries and often hid the tears. lula mae was more watcher and
listener now. yes, her emotions were still there, real & woman-
ly strong but they had failed her too often in the past, her
lovers had left memories that distorted her forehead and
scars that even she didn't want to acknowledge.

(pretty willie g left his fist print under her left ear, larry the
pimp provided her with a dislocated hip and baby frank left
her in $3000 debt with promises of short life if she mentioned
his whereabouts.)

lula mae now sought other signs of caring. she wanted rela-
tionships that were not so one-sided, short-termed or physi-
cally risky, she looked for verbal confirmation, evening phone
calls, unexpected love notes and deep back and foot mas-
sages at the day's end. lula mae, not yet 30, knew that she
was special, knew that her capacity for love was unusual and
also knew that the next man in her life would understand and
appreciate this specialness before he got any of it.

what will it be?
when will Blackmen learn that
fist & feet against the teeth
is like removing the heart of a people.
who will teach us
that slaps & kicks & verbal lashings
detour sharing, stop bonding,
destroy unifiers, retard respect & eliminate
connecting vision.
what will it be?
what messenger, what unmuted voice
will clarify touching
detail body contact without blackeyes?
what caller will articulate
disagreements without boxing,
love
without force.
where are the bold & rejuvenated men
and women that will head this most needed of
revolutionary struggles?

213

A MOTHER'S POEM

(for G.B.)

not often do we talk.
    destruction was to be mine at 28
    a bullet in the head   or
    wrong-handed lies that would lock
    me in pale cells that are designed to
    cut breathing and will.
you gave me maturity at daybreak
slashed my heart
and slowed the sprint toward extinction,
delayed my taking on the world alone,
you made living a laborious & loving commitment.

you shared new blood,
challenged mistaken vision,
suggested frequent smiles,
while enlarging life to more than
daily confrontations and lost battles
fought by unprepared poets.

not often did we talk.
your large acts of kindness shaped memory,
your caring penetrated bone & blood
and permanently sculptured a descendant.
i speak of you in smiles
and seldom miss a moment
to thank you for
saving a son.

214

Rainforest

you are forest   rain
dense with life green colors
forever pulling the blue of life into you
see you walk and
i would like to burst rainwater into you
swim in & out of you
opening you like anxious earthquakes
uncontrollable but beautiful & dangerous.

get with this woman   come
fire frozen beauty,
men cannot sleep around you
your presence demands attention
demands notice
demands touch & motion & communication.

you are runner
swift like warm wind hurricanes
fast like stolen firebirds
& you disrupt the silence in me
make me speak memories long forgotten & unshared.
secrets uttered in strange storms,
deep full sounds reserved for magical,
magical lovers.

listen runner
i have shared pain with you,
i have commented on future worlds to you,
i have let you touch the weak & strong of me,
i have tasted the tip of your ripeness &
kissed sweat from your middle.
i have bit into your mouth &
sucked the lifeforces from yr insides   and
i know you. understand you.
i have shared books & travel & music & growth with you.

sweet knows honey & i know you.
under salted water tides
& running against polluted earth
i've tried to be good to you woman
tried to care beyond words
        care beyond distant spaces
sensitive phases & quiet lies
care
beyond cruel music & false images.

you are original high & dream maker
& true men do not try to limit you.

listen woman black
i do not wish to dominate your dreams
or obstruct your vision.
trust my motion   feel
know that i am near and with you
& will cut the cold of winter winds to reach you.
you
are delicate bronze
in spring-summers and special autumns
you are   forest rain
dark & runner & hurricane-black
frequently
i say frequently i bring you
midnight   *rain.*

IN THE GUT OR GIVE ME FIVE

How many of you without doubt or hesitation can point out five Black men, locally or nationally, whose first priority is the liberation of Black people? How many of you can name five Black men right now, from the top of your head, who you believe under any circumstances, would not betray or sell out Black people for personal or political gain? Can you identify five true Black leaders who have not been compromised by money, white women, white privilege, oversized egos and media fame? Herein lies the legacy of our hurt. Serious and unbought Black men are few and fewer.

The century is not over. Let me issue this warning. Music comes in strange tones. The notes of our melodies are fast, slow and complexingly rhythmic. The songs of struggle must be unpredictable. The music players must constantly practice and continuously train body and mind. To become accomplished music makers there is but one method for serious preparation: study, train, practice, strive to tone the physical with the mental and the spiritual so that they function as one. Be reliable and proactive.

Study your strengths and weaknesses. Know your body like sweet knows honey. Keep yourself lean, hard and ready for war. Deeply examine the way of life. We must erase the landscapes of fear and inaction. Atlanta and Buffalo are still with us. Black life in America is cheap and according to the world-runners, highly dispensable. Hear me well. There are white men (and women) in this country (and the world) who see as their God-given task, the effective neutralization of the Black movement, which at its base means the systematic destruction of Black boys and men. Violent aggression against Black men is nothing new; however, what is most revealing is that the current aggression against Blacks is taking place after two decades of "so-called" Black advancement. Only the critically weak-minded can fail to see the picture on the screen.

Active, consistent and effective Black struggle is our only *oasis*. As we travel the desert of our time, take a few

217

minutes during the day to listen to the heartbeat of our children, stop often and look into their eyes, survey their smiles (if they are there) and ask yourself this question: *Do I want my children to be crippled zombies, incapable of decision or movement, totally dependent on the chief criminals of the world for their survival and development?* If the answer is *yes,* simply go back to sleep. If your answer is *NO,* quietly yet quickly start to transform your life. Critically assess the Word (study), don't give quarter or comfort to the enemy, learn to hide tears and anger with smiles and planning. Above all, believe, in the gut, that we can—Black men and women—create a better, better world.

THE DESTRUCTION OF FATHERS

at the beginning he felt that it gave him
                              time
to do the acts of importance that somehow
he was unable to do   before
the vacating of rooms   before
the clearing of book shelves & dresser drawers
before the
greed of lawyers
tears of children   and
draining sleeplessness of fathers.

divorce generated an abundance of
                      time
to hear,
to contemplate the missing   the mistakes
                       time
to seek pure noise,
for self-inflicted wounds,
planned interruptions,
& suicidal waiting moments   for
wishing & rushing of weekend visits

at thirty-eight it was a devastating   time
to have lost wife, children and familiar spaces
to "irreconcilable differences,"
obsolete definitions & rapid-firing mouth.

again
it was a devastating   time with only
quiet to debate at whether men should
share in garbage-emptying, floor-mopping,
dish-washing, laundry-doing, shopping, &c.
when one is alone there are no questions
only time
and clarity arriving
too late.

POET: FOR LARRY NEAL

in time and time
in evening nights
in quiet search and final answer
they took the poets away

they promised them gifts of gifts and portable and
    lasting fame
they promised them beautiful life, hungerless days,
    rising riches
and lasting lust. they promised gold & university chairs
    & unlimited
publication.

they promised promises
and
in return
they suggested that the poets
sing a
falsesong.

this world is full of
missing,
and dying
& unpublished
poets.

My Brothers

my brothers i will not tell you
who to love or not love
i will only say to you
that
Black women have not been
loved enough.

i will say to you
that
we are at war & that
Black men in america are
being removed from the
earth
like loose sand in a wind storm
and that the women Black are
three to each of us.

no
my brothers i will not tell you
who to love or not love
but
i will make you aware of our
self-hating and hurting ways.
make you aware of whose bellies
you dropped from.
i will glue your ears to those images
you reflect which are not being
loved.

The Damage We Do

he loved his women
weak & small
so that he would not tire
of
beating them.
he sought the weakest & the smallest
so that they couldn't challenge
his rage of boxing
their heads up against refrigerators,
slamming their hands in doors,
stepping on them like roaches,
kicking them in their centers of life.
all of his women
were
weak and small and sick
& he an
embarrassment to the human form
was not an exception in america.

RAPE: THE MALE CRIME

there are mobs & strangers
in us
who scream of the women
wanted and
will get
as if the women are ours for the
taking.

our mothers, sisters, wives and
daughters ceased to be the
women men want   we think of them as
loving family   music & soul   bright wondermints.
they are not locker room talk
not the hunted lust or   dirty
cunt burnin hoes.
bright wondermints are excluded   by association as
blood & heart   bone & memory
& we will destroy a rapist's knee caps,
& write early grave on his thoughts
to protect them.

it will do us large to recall
when the animal in us rises
that all women are someone's
mother, sister, wife or daughter
and are not fruit to be stolen when hungry.

a significant few of their
fathers, brothers, husbands, sons
and growing strangers
are willing to unleash harm on the earth
and spill blood in the eyes
of
maggots in running shoes
who do not know the sounds of birth
or respect the privacy of the human form.

WHITE ON BLACK CRIME

lately and not by choice
milton washington is self employed.
workin hard
he collects aluminum cans,
pop bottles, papers & cardboard
and sells them to the
local recycling center.

milton washington is an unemployed
master welder who has constantly sought
work in & out of his trade.
he is now seen on beaches, in parks,
in garbage cans, leaving well-lit alleys
in the evenings pushing one cart
& pulling the other, head to the side
eyes glued southward long-steppin homeward.

milton's unemployment ran out 14 months ago.
first the car went & he questioned his manhood.
next the medical insurance, savings & family
nights out ceased & he questioned his god.
finally his home was snatched & he disappeared
for 2 days & questioned his dreams
and all he believed in.

milton works a 15 hour day &
recently redefined his life for
the 6th time selecting as his only goal
the housing, feeding & keeping of his family
together.

yesterday the payout per pound
on aluminum was reduced by 1/4 cent
as the stock market hit an all-time high
& the president smiled through a speech
on economic recovery, welfare cheats & the
availability of jobs for those who want to work.

milton washington has suffered
the humiliation of being denied food stamps,
the laughter and cat calls of children,
the misunderstanding in the eyes of his family
and friends.
milton believed in the american way
even hung flags on the 4th & special days
and demanded the respect of god & country in
his home.

at 1/4 cent reduction in pay per pound
milton washington will have to add
an hour and a half to his 15 hour day.
milton washington, more american than black,
quiet and resourceful, a collector of dreams
cannot close his eyes anymore,
cannot excuse the failure in his heart,
cannot expect miracles in daylight,
is real close, very, very close to hurtin somebody
real bad.

A Poem for Quincy Jones, Sidney Poitier, Harry Belafonte, Kareem Abdul-Jabbar, James Earl Jones, Wilt Chamberlain, Richard Pryor, Redd Foxx, Lou Rawls, &c., &c., &c. for Days

it is actual and prophetic   that
when the money comes
when the fame and autograph seekers arrive,
when there is something to share & wear,
that the *root* is forced into basements,
backrooms and aching embarrassment.

acts toward the indigenous become frigid clichés
(after children wrecking & torturous, rise to the pinnacle)
the *root* is now tolerated baggage & excessive worry,
a for real style cramper & potential court warrior.
for him the current revelation is that
"people are just people"
converting the universe into one gigantic lovefest.
exempting
the berrycolored   nappyheaded   rustykneed
exempting
the widehipped   biglipped   cherrybrown women.

his eyes have gone pink sucking
venom from the people
who less than a word ago
less than a few missed meals ago
used his ass as a shoe shiner.
        tap tap dance do the bounce now
        do the white boy richard 357 magnum yr car
        shoot death in yr toe freebase raw brilliance
        fire up tap tap tap dance run out da pain in da
           brain.

stardom is the ultimate drug,
fame fogs tradition   dismembers values
& elevates egos to cocaine highs.
idol status
is volcanic to the insides   evaporates memory
& neutralizes kindness.
the *root*
the unbought memory of the culture
flows red in the women.
when the women are traded and reduced to
matrilineal burning bitches
bleeding sets in   families decay
rendering generational destruction
producing final stop orders.

ask your momma.

COMIN STRONG

and where are the men Black and ready?
some say,
they've lost their way
beneath pig's litter & fool's gold.
others say,
they are hid under political deception
& three dollar bills returning in numbers
as colored traitors clothed in abundance.

the real word is that the men have become
pregnant with spoiled food
& thoughts of false grandeur.
they drive boat-cars,
smoke strange weeds,
destroy their noses with crippling dust,
manicure their nails
& talk wrong about their women.
some say,
it is best that these men stay lost.

the new men Black
do not measure themselves in
the way of the elusive streets
do not look toward the west as the test.
the new men Black with dust & dirt
are clear thinkers and city learned
are not tied to garbage cans & whiskey breath.
these men take their sons seriously &
listen closely to their daughters.
they do not come as beggars or buyers
they are teachers and doers returning in
a force that's unimaginable.

the new men Black are
tongue silent, hawkeyed and dangerous.
many who should know say
that these men do not play,
do not pass blank checks.
they say that these men cannot be
bought.

MESSAGE TO OUR SONS

son,
do not forget the women killed
by the whites & men negro made white.
do not disregard the women Black
killed for closing their legs to
bodies foreign to their insides,
for preserving the culture of their foreparents,
for daring to be the just.
son, let your memory not erase
or betray the sacred teachings of
these   women.   mothers,   sisters,   lovers   and   wives
whom the world has transgressed against.
record their tracks in code and memory.
my son do not neglect our women nor
forgive those who have *violated*
a precious part of you.

FOR BLACKMEN
WITH INTEGRITY AND CONVICTIONS

there are people beyond clout and distance
who have orders
from above   on high   to do you
debilitating harm
worse than broken knee caps and twisted face
worse than ruining your good name or destroying your
    marriage
worse than turning your friends and people against
    you.

they have final stop orders
these people have cleaned weapons,
sharpened skills,
have mapped your every movement,
booked your weaknesses & dissected your strengths
you are a considerable foe
& many are preparing to exterminate you with
"extreme prejudice"

their design
is to close the history books on your name,
crown you traitor & child molestor.
anything
to erase the people's positive memory of you.

it will be difficult to brace
against this storm.

continue as you must
intensify and insulate
let them know that
they're in for a fight.

Get Fired Up

get fired up
get excited about hue and dark colors
ignite truth in the temple
there will be many who will try to take you out
watch the light shadows
exemplify & scream cleanliness into the world
leave yr mark
the children must know that you
& you   & you
carried the message.

Hanging Hard in America

one does not want to hurt   the word is that
bodies break easily in the west   the word is that
the important articles are made of plastic & glue
put together by people whose major aim is
profit:
        made in japan is no longer laughable
        enter hong kong, taiwan, singapore, &c.,
        to buy american is not quality its patriotic,
        the way is buy now pay if you catch me,
        get it now tomorrow may be never,
        pay for what you want beg for the needs.

families are disappearing.
children & vegetation are back seated
& automobiles and canned foods are the
measurements of normalcy. family bonding
or preparing for the long hike is what the crazy do.
lips thunder everywhere talking in tongues praising
"my god" & intellectual pursuits like reading & thinking
are left to fools, bureaucrats, compromising scholars
& a few starving & unlettered poets.

the urgent quests are for new money markets,
i. magnum & neiman marcus accounts.
it is taught that light shines on those who can
afford electricity & new definitions depend on your
politics and cash flow:
right means don't do it,
integrity translates as square,
honesty is lonely,
the rich are correct,
the poor are lazy,
loyalty is rewards in suitcases after dark &
the world is never too small for liars,
only for amateurs. were you not told that
professionals do not fabricate the truth they become

233

historians and anthropologists & reinterpret reality.
so we hurt,
we learn to hate as we dig in
for the long track.
as should be our ancestors speak wisdom:
do not send your children to be taught by
those who do not love them;
raise strong, loving and sane children and
we will not have to repair broken adults.
above all the final call is:
do not forgive violation of people & loss of language,
do not forget dirt in the eye & the middle passage.

AMERICA: THE FUTURE

in a country

where pride is measured
in body counts

a black
school aged boy
pledged
allegiance to the flag

as the words came
he
thought about today's
ball game
& about the
homeruns he would hit
& his special willie mays catch

he didn't remember the flag
until after
he noticed the
canceled sign on the ball park's gate

that night he asked
his momma:
    "momma why the flag got holes in it?"
her reply:
    "daddy's back."

BIKO

water dripping   drop by drop
into the ears of the broederbond*
leaving them waterlogged and senseless
desperately appreciating pain.
knowing the displacement of dreams
knowing what slavery is and raw smiles of Black
          mommas
following husbands to shanty towns to squat in
          squalor & mud is.

to be born among apologists
in a land taken from one's ancestors
is a profound comment on how far
we have lost our way.

to be born among weaker apologies
from color men in white collars
who constantly preach "a better day a comin,"
tomorrow

expect tennis and cricket,
jogging, handball & polo played on manicured greens.
better days of beer and evening playgrounds
and admission to divinity schools.
but never   never
the retrieval of one's land.

as the young   young men & women
steal away into the heat of the heart
seeking the uncompromising past in search of
clear sight inciting the alerting question,
"why did they kill Steve Biko?"
their message to Black america,
"don't send us no ribbons to wear."

*The white brotherhood that once held exclusive power in South Afrika.

SUN AND STORM

beyond weep and whisper,
beyond clown and show,
beyond why & where & not now
clear the voices

there is *storm* on the horizon.
beneath calm & cold & killer death
there is *vision* approaching.
beneath filth & fear & running asses
there is planning & hope & connecting trust.
beneath traffic stops and sex crazed negroes
there are new people arising
clothed in love & work & a will to advance.

newpeople
bold and sure   tested tough   fever wise
these are womenblack with brain and womb &
smiles that regenerate.
these are menblack with mind and seed &
strength of strength.
they are children-conscious and elder-wise
sweet lovers of life.
newpeople
known in afrika,
known in asia,
known in europe & the americas
with their rainbow smiles, willing minds,
and bridge-building backs as the
people of the sun.

End Notes

if parting is necessary
part as lovers.
part as two people
who can still
smile & talk & share
the good & important
with each other.
part
wishing the other
happy
happy life
in a world
fighting against the
beautiful,
fighting against the
men & women,
sisters and brothers
Black as
we.

FUTURE

first
it is between the black and the black
come
not as empty earth,
not as wasted energy,
not as apologetic color consciousness,
not as fool blinded to light,
not as imitation cardboard.

come
as gifted lovers
eyes bright & daring life.
come
as ripening fruit
quick smiles and joyous words.
come
woman to man
man to woman
pursuing the way of life
within the colors of vision
between the
black and the black.

EARTHQUAKES

(for Frances Cress Welsing)

in the hot of the eye
at the insertion of cayenne
what really matters is:
children catching breath,
children experiencing love and continuation,
children understanding the good and emerging evil,
children expecting a future,
children smiling quickly and uninhibited
in this world.
        as the smiles cease conflict beckons
        hearts hurt   blood rushes   hands sweat
        pain ensues and comes like pins in the spine
understand this:
conscious men do not make excuses
do not expect their women to carry their water,
harvest the food and prepare it too.
world over it is known that
breast sucking is only guaranteed to babies.
        sisters if the men do not fight,
        if the men are not responsible
cover the breast   close the legs   stop the love
cancel good times   erase privileges   question man-
        hood.

if the men engage the enemy
get ready for rumor & divisive headaches
everyone will want to know their price,
traitors will try & confirm that the men can be
        bought,
enemies will pass gold to family & lovers to buy his
        dreams.
if the engaged men are of the wise kind
they will appreciate the greater needs and
without doubt or hesitation tell them our pay back is:
georgia, the states of florida & alabama, we want
  texas.

when the smiles quit when the laughter quiets
conflict beckons   hearts hurt   blood rushes
        hands sweat
spine strengthens   & brothers comprehend.
catch the sun & get on up
rise on the run. open eyed
ready & expecting danger

expecting earthquakes.

SUN RISE MISSIONS

(for Hoyt W. Fuller)

He will be missed, not lost among papers,
remembered in midnight study cells
and early morning runs.
remembered as an originator of
wisdom
from a vision that was sound & sane
steadfast and tempered
Tempo between songs and dance   between
fist and articulation   call him
screamingly dangerous

Sang beauty first
notice the eyes of children
locate their living & eating space
try & smile now.
run with & against the common wind
do damage for damage be
unpredictable with map and compass
& weapons pressed against the cheek

Catch fire & fire
notice
there is an uneasiness among us
window shades are drawn,
people talk in nods and whispers
babies are again born in homes,
people are picking up books and nails
and anxiously listening to grandparents.
there is sunrise on the horizon
Pass this word quickly and quietly
there are rats in the streets.

Poison is needed. Now.

DESTINY

under volcanoes & timeless years within watch
and low tones. around corners, in deep caves among
misunderstood and sometimes meaningless sounds.
cut beggars, outlaw pimps & whores. resurrect work.
check your distance blue
come
earthrise men deepblack and ready
come
sunbaked women rootculture on the move.

just do what you're suppose to do
just do what you say you gonta do
not the impossible,
not the unimaginative,
not copy clothed as original and surely
not bitter songs in european melodies.

take hold
do the necessary, the possible, the correctly simple
take hold
talk of missions & interpret destiny
put land and selfhood on the minds of our people
do the expected,
do what all people do

reverse destruction.
capture tomorrows.

8
KILLING MEMORY,
SEEKING ANCESTORS
(1987)

Getting to this Place

I have had the privilege to travel far and deep into other cultures. Any kind of travel to the imaginative mind is both rewarding and challenging. Travel can also be painful to the culturally sensitive; for example, it is extremely difficult to enjoy oneself in Haiti and in certain parts of Afrika. Afrika entered my consciousness in 1960 and there has not been a day that I have not considered my relationship to that vast and complex continent.

I first went to Afrika in 1969 to attend the first Pan-Afrikan Festival in Algeria. After a decade of serious struggle in the United States for Black self-determination, my visit to Afrika was crucial to my cultural development. I went looking for answers. The past ten years in the U.S. had been an intense period of struggle and study during which my generation fought to rid itself of a colonial-slave-centered mindset. My first trip to Afrika was instructive, but after seven visits to North, East, and West Afrika, I am still fighting with my questions. My searchings have also taken me to the West Indies, Europe, Asia, and South America. However, as a man of Afrikan foreparents, the land of the sun has a special meaning for me.

Youth has its own naivety. I long ago lost my innocence in the concrete of Detroit and the mud of Arkansas. Yet, I was still not prepared for the land that gave birth to civilization.

My personal journals eat into my poetry. It is in poetry that I have learned to communicate best. After fourteen books published in a twenty-one year period, I have become a poet. I now feel comfortable with the description *poet* or *writer*. America has a way of forcing even the strongest into denying reality. Afrika demanded reentry.

In all of my work I've tried to give the readers melodies and songs that foster growth and questions. I wanted my readers to become a more informed and better people. I think that my experiences have made me a better person; I would like to think that I am a good and productive one also. That is partially what I am working for. Study, work, travel, and struggle have taught me not to take myself too seriously, but to be serious enough so that others, especially my enemies, do not mistake love and caring for weakness.

Moving culturally from negro to Black to Afrikan to Afrikan American has been quite a trip. I *never* had to get "high" because my quest for knowledge (i.e., truth) carried with it a multiplicity of altitudes and attitudes. Progressive thinking and acting in most of the world can get one killed. This is what Afrika and Afrikan American struggle, in a highly abbreviated form, has taught me:

1. Before doing what I say, see what I do.
2. Good words are healthy, but deeds are what bring the food, clothe and house the children, and build tomorrows.
3. When one is full, it is easy to criticize the hungry.
4. It is easier to believe than to think.
5. What is increasingly rare among Western people is friendship and caring.
6. Honesty and moral consciousness practiced among the people has a greater impact than sharp-witted demagoguery.
7. Ideas run the world.
8. Force is both an idea and a reality.
9. Children first, which means that family is pre-children.
10. That which is truly valuable cannot be bought.
11. Freedom is only given to people who do not understand it.
12. Greed disguised as need is a great enemy.
13. Do not surround yourself with people who always say yes.
14. Knowledge is non-decaying food, and study brings a vast harvest to those who partake of it.
15. A people that runs from the truth will never know beauty and will sleep with lies.
16. The only ignorant question is the one not asked.
17. One's culture is one's life.
18. Values based upon tradition, reason, and practice are not negotiable and memory is knowledge.
19. Listening is to learning as water is to life.
20. Seeking beauty in relationships is as life-giving as the juice of carrots and the morning sun.

There is much more, but let me stop here; brevity is respected.

I have acquired a healthy skepticism; however, as many can attest, it is still easy to get to my heart. What is missing among Afrikan American people is vision. Many of our people think and act in a way that is embarrassing to the normal mind. However, in much of the world, the abnormal still defines normality.

It is a 24-hour-a-day job to be a conscious Afrikan in America (or the world) where the mass media hourly project anti-Black images. This is why a people's culture is critical to its development. It was Long and Collier who stated in their book, *Afro-American Writing*, that "Definitions are increasingly important. The survival of culture—any culture—depends in large measure on the nature of its definitions of itself and of those aspects of life on which its survival depends: for example, what the past implies, what freedom means, who the enemy is. The literature of a culture is a totality of the definitions, a self-portrait of that culture. Knowledge of a literature, then, yields valuable insight into the culture that produced it."

We are summertime people; therefore, it is not so odd that we act funny in this environment. However, the world is changing rapidly and we must ride with the tide as we try to humanize it. Question everything, study, study, and study some more. Smile often, stay clean, and seek beauty. Try not to be judgmental and petty in your actions. As the brothers say, "Stay up," and I will add: Keep struggling; stay strong and aware, too. To kill the people's memory is to remove them from history and future, but when the people believe in and act positively and passionately on such beliefs, only their children and the land will live longer.

H.R.M.
September, 1986

249

KILLING MEMORY

(For Nelson and Winnie Mandela)

the soul and fire of windsongs must not be neutral
cannot be void of birth and dying
wasted life
locked
in the path of vicious horrors
masquerading
as progress and spheres of influence

what of mothers
without milk of willing love,
of fathers
whose eyes and vision
have been separated from feelings of earth and growth,
of children
whose thoughts dwell
on rest and food and
human kindness?

Tomorrow's future rains in
atrocious mediocrity and suffering deaths.

in america's america the excitement is over
a rock singer's glove and burning hair
as serious combat rages over
prayer in schools,
the best diet plan,
and women
learning how to lift weights
to the rhythms of
"what's love got to do with it?"

ask the children,
always the children caught in the
absent spaces of adult juvenility
all
breakdancing and singing to

"everything is everything" while
noise occupies the mind as
garbage feeds the brain.

in el salvador mothers search for their sons
and teach their daughters the way of the knife.

in south afrika mothers bury hearts without bodies
while pursuing the secrets of forgotten foreparents.

in afghanistan mothers claim bones and teeth from
mass graves and curse the silent world.

in lebanon the sons and daughters receive horror hourly
sacrificing childhood for the promise of land.

in ethiopia mothers separate wheat from the desert's dust
while the bones of their children cut through dried skin.

tomorrow's future
may not belong to the people,
may not belong to dance or music
where
getting physical is not an exercise but
simply translates into people working,
people fighting,
people enduring insults and smiles,
enduring crippling histories and black pocket politics
wrapped in diseased blankets
bearing AIDS markings in white,
destined for victims that do not question
gifts from strangers
do not question
love of enemy.
who owns the earth?
most certainly not the people,
not the hands that work the waterways,
nor the backs bending in the sun,
nor the boned fingers soldering transistors,

Killing Memory, Seeking Ancestors

not the legs walking the massive fields,
nor the knees glued to pews of storefront or granite churches
nor the eyes blinded by computer terminals,
not the bloated bellies on toothpick legs
all victims of decisions
made at the washington monument and lenin's tomb
by aged actors viewing
red dawn and the *return of rambo part IX.*

tomorrow
may not belong to the
women and men laboring,
hustling,
determined to avoid contributing
to the wealth
of gravediggers from foreign soil
& soul.
determined to stop the erosion
of indigenous music
of building values
of traditions.

memory is only precious if
you have it.

memory is only functional
if it works for you.
people
of colors and voices
are locked in multibasement state buildings
stealing memories
more efficient
than vultures tearing flesh
from
decaying bodies.

the order is that the people are to
believe and believe
questioning or contemplating

---

the direction of the weather is
unpatriotic.

it is not that we distrust poets and politicians.

we fear the disintegration of thought,
we fear the cheapening of language,
we fear the history of victims and the loss of vision,
we fear writers whose answer to
maggots drinking from the open
wounds of babies
is
to cry genocide while demanding
ten cents per word and
university chairs.
we fear politicians
that sell coffins at a discount
and consider ideas blasphemy
as young people world over bleed from the teeth while
aligning themselves with whoever
brings the food.
whoever brings love.

who speaks the language of
bright memory?

who speaks the language of
necessary memory?

the face of poetry must be fire erupting volcanoes,
hot silk forging new histories,
poetry delivering light greater than barricades of silence,
poetry dancing, preparing seers, warriors, healers
and parents beyond the age of babies,
poetry delivering melodies that cure dumbness & stupidity
yes, poets uttering to the intellect and spirit,
screaming to the genes and environments
revitalizing the primacy of the word and world.
poets must speak the language of the rain,

decipher the message of the sun,
play the rhythms of the earth,
demand the cleaning of the atmosphere,
carry the will and way of the word,
feel the heart and questions of the people
and be conditioned and ready
to move.

to come
at midnight or noon

to run
against the monied hurricane in this
the hour of forgotten selves,
forgiven promises
and
frightening whispers
of rulers in heat.

254

THE UNION OF TWO

(For Ife and Jake)

What matters is the renewing and long running kinship
seeking common mission, willing work, memory, melody,
        song.

marriage is an art,
created by the serious, enjoyed by the mature,
watered with morning and evening promises.

those who grow into love
remain anchored
like egyptian architecture and seasonal flowers.

it is afrikan that woman and man join in smile, tears, future.
it is traditional that men and women share expectations,
        celebrations, struggles.
it is legend that the nations start in the family.
it is afrikan that our circle expands.
it is wise that we believe in tomorrows, children, quality.
it is written that our vision will equal the promise.

so that your nation will live and tell your stories accurately,
you must be endless in your loving touch of each other,
your unification is the message,
continuance the answer.

                                          August 7, 1986

Possibilities: Remembering Malcolm X

it was not that you were pure.
your contradictions were small wheels,
returning to the critical questions:

    what is good?
    what does it mean to be black?
    what is wise?
    what is beautiful?
    where are the women and men of honor?
    what is a moral-ethical consciousness?
    where will our tomorrows be?
    what does a people need to mature?

it was your search and doings
that separated you from puppets.
"a man lives as a man does"

if you lived among the committed
this day how would you lead us?

what would be your strength,
the word, the example, both?

would you style in thousand
dollar suits and false eye glasses?

would you kneel at the feet of arabs
that raped your grandmother?

would you surround yourself with
zombies in bow ties, zombies with parrot tongues?

it was not that you were pure.
the integrity of your vision and pain,
the quality of your heart and decision
confirmed your caring for local people, and your
refusal to assassinate progressive thought
has carved your imprint on the serious.

ABERRATIONS

(hair, color and quiet desperation in the last quarter of the
20th century post-1986 and it is still political to, consciously or
    unconsciously,
desire hair that is straight or curly in the fashion of europe
and to seek the lightest and "fairest" of people to love while
proclaiming one's deepest and undying commitment to
    all that is black, and on paper, beautiful.)

the utter pain of being dark
and woman,
living among men who despise
the "nappiness" of head & the
hue of skin sunbaked before birth.

the unimaginable hurt of being dark
and short and man,
living among images of vikings
tall and conquering
"angel-like" roaming the earth
seeding the wombs of the vanquished coloreds.

the war was fought
when being natural became anti-self & unkind,
the war was confusing
when we lied to ourselves to convince
the nonbelief in us,
the war was in disorder
when practice became embarrassing,
the war was lost
when self-hatred emerged as a force greater than the
scorn of sworn enemies.

beauty and being beautiful is not the question.
all people desire beauty.
a full people needs love,
music and flowers in their lives.
whose love remands the answer?

Killing Memory, Seeking Ancestors

whose music determines the call?
whose beauty decides the winner?
whose culture dictates the dance?

what is the color and texture of your flower?

THE END OF WHITE WORLD SUPREMACY

The day, hour, minute
and
second that the
chinese
and
japanese
sign
a
joint
industrial
and
mililary
pact.

Searching

1.

Sisters
in moonlight and after
beautiful women speak in tongues and
answers.

where is the music?
where is the passionate fire promised?
running
with the men—loudly,
backward and fisted
fastly and crudely becoming the
enemy of silence,
enemy of love and vision.

friend of despair and destruction
tonight and often
many and more of the womenblack are
alone
and searching with children
some
creating networks of hatred
for the limitations in their lives
robbed of laughter and joy
challenged by biology and babies
as the men
keep company with others and themselves.

2. Empty warriors

the men,
occupying bedrooms and unemployment lines, on corners, in
bars, stranded between middle management and bankruptcy,
caught in warped mindsets of "success in america," the kind
taught to first generation immigrants at local trade schools
and jr. colleges, taught to people lost and unaware of history
or future, ignorant of the middle passages.

the men,
occupying space with men and motives, in prisons, in safe
houses, shooting up with juice and junk, many with hairless
noses and needle-marked toes, searching for missing history,
searching for the when and how of "making it in america,"

the men
escaped and taken, twice and three times absorbed in life
and sharing, absorbed in locating the mission and magic, the
manner and muscle, the answer and aims, walking the bor-
ders between smiles and outrage.

3. Transitions

in moonlight and after,
beautiful women,

respected women become elders of the storm,
riders of the hurricane,
keepers of the volcano,
warm and worked,
caught and embittered
often blaming
themselves for misery planned before their birth,
for hurt conceived by slaveholders on wall street,
executed prior to foreparents' arrival to consciousness.

4. Arrivals

of the women clean and cured,
of the men sensitive and sound,
all focused and calm,
listeners of a distant wind
love full and wanted
they
did not wait
& knew in the aloneness of early hours
that
snow was temporary and transient
     understood that evil could not be conquered
     on knees with folded hands,
     understood that ten decades of
     colorless rice, enriched bread and sugar
     would weaken a people,
     understood too that slavery, if it is to work,
     has to be accepted by the enslaved.
snow is temporary and heat does boil water.

263

5. The gathering

gathering as they do with
their water and weather,

their heat and blankets,
their thoughts and hearts,
wrapping their children and songs
in the mysteries of their men being butchered
beyond recognition.
some rushing
to the wilderness of
urban consumption and corporate takeovers,
in the midnight of a wasted culture of pornographic values,
in the indecisions of life and loving.
others coming with care
seeking
quality in the confusion of mistaken loyalties,
demanding
quality of responses,
quality in the searching,
quality in the giving and loving,
quality in the receiving
beginning anew.
        fresh.

264

POET: GWENDOLYN BROOKS AT 70

as in muslc,
as in griots singing,
as in language mastered, matured
beyond melodic roots.

you came from the land of ivory and vegetation,
of seasons with large women guarding secrets.
your father was a running mountain,
your mother a crop-gatherer and God-carrier,
your family, earthgrown waterfalls,
all tested, clearheaded, focused.
ready to engage.

centuries displaced in this land of denial and disbelief,
this land of slavery and sugar diets,
of bacon breakfasts, short suns and long moons,
you sought memory and hidden ideas,
while writing the portrait or a battered people.

artfully you avoided becoming a literary museum,
side-stepped retirement and canonization,
gently casting a rising shadow over a generation of
urgent-creators waiting to make fire,
make change.

with the wind in your hand,
as in trumpeter blowing,
as in poet singing,
as in sister of the people, of the language,
smile at your work.

your harvest is coming in, bountifully.

MAGNIFICENT TOMORROWS

(For Queen Mother Moore, Karima White, Sonia Sanchez, Mari Evans,
Ruby Dee, Assata Shakur, Julia Fields and Janet Sankey)

1.
flames from sun
fire in during rainbow nights.

the women are colors of earth and ocean—
earth as life,
the beginning waters,
magnificent energy.

as the women go, so go the people,
determining mission,
determining possibilities.

stopping the women stops the future.
to understand slavery, feel the eyes of mothers.
there lies hope even in destruction, lies unspeakable horror or
fruitful destiny.

we
are now in the europe of our song,
non-melody with little beat or hope.
current dreams are visionless,
producing behavior absent of greatness.

2.
without great teachings,
without important thoughts,
without significant deeds,
the ordinary emerges as accepted example
gluing the women
to kitchens,
afternoon soaps
and the limiting imagination of sightless men.
producing
a people that move with the
quickness of decapitated bodies
while
calling such movement
divine.

possibilities: listen to the wind of women, the voices of big
mama, zora neale, sister rosa, fanny lou, pretty renee, gwen
brooks, queen nzinga and warrior mothers. all birth and
prophecy, black and heart warm, bare and precise. the
women detailing the coming collapse or rise. the best and
bent of youth emerging. telling triumphantly. if we listen, if we
feel & prepare.

267

3.
if black women do not love,
there is no love.
if black women do not love,
harmony and sustaining humanity cease.
if black women do not love,
strength disconnects.
families sicken. growth is questionable &
there are few reasons to conquer ideas or foe.

as black women love,
europe gives way to southern meals.
as black women mature,
so come flames from sun,
rainbows at dusk.
sculpture of elizabeth catlett and
music of nina simone.
as womenblack connect,
the earth expands, minds open and books reveal the possible
if we study
if we feel the flow & secrets of our women,
if we listen,
if we concentrate,
if we carefully care,
if we simply do.

ALWAYS REMEMBER WHERE YOU ARE

(For Zora Neale Hurston)

1.
it seems as though she had been
planted outside northwestern high
next to the basketball court on 86th street
behind her weather-worn blue buick
seated on a rusting folding
chair where she sold cookies, candies, history,
causes, chewing gum, vision, corn chips,
soda pop and advice to teenagers with
26-year-old mothers and grandmothers
under 40. most of their father's music
ceased during viet nam and the fbi's
war against black men who dared to
question the saintliness of congress and the
imperial presidency.

269

Killing Memory, Seeking Ancestors

2.

She sold wisdom from her weather
worn buick bought for her by her son,
a former NBA basketball star. he had
earned NBA records and money in new york
during the 60s and 70s flying high above
hoops and reality only to slip on a
nickel bag and later fall into deadly
habit of sniffing his breakfast, lunch
and dinner. eventually his snacks interrupted
practice and games as his place in
the world became that of a certified
junky circling a basketball that
he could not bounce and a mother
he could not recognize, nor she him.

270

3.
As his records faded and his money
disappeared quicker than shit in
a flushing toilet, he returned home to
mamma, a pitiful casuality, unable
to write his name or remember the
love that got him out of dusable high
with scholarship offers from 50
universities, no questions asked.
that his mother cared and he was 1st team
all american high school and college is
now history. this mother, in the august
and winter of her time, with eyes
and smile frozen in urban memories,
sells sugar and dreams now from the
trunk of destroyed promises in america.

POEM RESULTING FROM A TELEVISION AD
FOR *THE COLOR PURPLE*

Girl
"you sho is ugly,"
broken too,
auctioned off.
sold and resold again & again
prostituted by
negroes passing & modern slavemasters
who smell gold,
smell VCR royalties,
smell cable TV rentals,
smell negroes willing to kneel, and suck again.

knowing that women "ugly" and non-ugly, "dumb" and
   undumb, daily at
typing pools, day-care centers, laundrymats, card parties,
   avon lunches,
factory assembly lines and tupperware picnics share horror
   stories of
their lives with men and will dress in sunday's best to stand in
   minus 14
degree wind chill premiers to see themselves beaten and
   humiliated to
confirm fact and rumor of rough life and the insightfulness of
   d.w. griffith's *birth of a nation*.

the women of good words,
the women of history and content,
the women of balance,
the women who enjoy their men
are either lucky, lying or crazy.

272

lucky?
these women knew that black people didn't walk on water or
        come to
america first class twa.
to be in america is not luck but is a
little told chronicle of continental rape and hate.

lying?
the lie that america was bought
from indians on the trail of 1000 tears & that
colored people loved plantation life and
trees exist to hang black men from regardless of the
utterings of amos & andy, stepin fetchit and quincy jones.

crazy, black people who refuse to mentally die
or buy are crazy. elijah muhammad, martin luther king,
malcolm x were complete aberrations & crazy.
crazy. paul robeson. triple crazy.
harriet tubman, fannie lou hamer, southern crazy.
marcus garvey, edward blyden, claude mckay
south of florida caribbean crazy.
margaret danner, larry neal, hoyt w. fuller, literary crazy.
bob marley, bessie smith, marvin gaye,
musically, musically crazy, crazy before contact with
        europeans crazy,
black people who refuse to mentally
die or buy into america's
nightmare are positively
crazy.

WOMAN WITH MEANING

she is small and round,
round face and shoulders connected to half-sun breast,
on a round stomach that sits on rounded buttocks,
held up by short curved legs and circular feet,
her smile reveals bright teeth, and when it comes,
her eyes sing joy and her face issues in gladness,
she is brilliant beauty.

she likes colors,
her hair, which is worn in its natural form, is
often accented with vivid, cheerful scarfs. her make-up
is difficult to detect, it complements her oak-colored skin,
suggesting statuesque music. her scent is fresh mango
and moroccan musk. her clothes are like haitian paintings,
highly noticeable during her rhythmic walks,
as she steps like a dancer.

she is a serious woman,
her values,
her ideas,
her attitudes,
her actions are those of a reflective mind.
her child is her life,
her people their future,
she and her child live alone and the brothers
speak good words about them.

the brothers,
married and unmarried, want to help her.
it is difficult to be with her and not
lose one's sense of balance,
one's sense of place and wisdom.
that is what caring does.
her aloneness
hurts and tears at the inside of serious men.
some of the older men have tried

to tie her heart into theirs but
the commitment was never enough.
her sense of honor and history,
her knowing of sisterhood and rightness
force her to sleep alone each night.

the brothers
continue to speak good words about her,
many
when thinking of
her smile.
others light candles and pray.
some send her notes, gifts and poems,
all
hoping for the unexpected.

HOYT W. FULLER: NO EASY COMPROMISES

There is something magical about a person who has a passion for ideas. A part of the magic is that he or she is usually very serious and is a person with high standards and a definable purpose for living that is far beyond the ordinary. If such a person is willing and able to share his love—and in doing so, change others for the better—he needs to be remembered. Hoyt W. Fuller lived ahead of his time and, as is often the case of visionaries, he was impatient with mediocrity and ignorance. Yet, within the imperfections of growing up in America, he shared his music and mission with us to the end of his bright and influential life.

Hoyt Fuller's work influenced a generation of young scholars, activists, poets, teachers, writers and thinkers. His voice, quiet and consistent as editor of the important *Black World* (*Negro Digest*) and *First World* magazines, introduced Afro-American and African literature and writers to an international audience. His book, *Journey to Africa*, set the tone for a serious consideration and contemplation of that massive and complex continent. As teacher (adjunct professor at Northwestern and Cornell universities) and editor, he brought clarity to the turbulent decades of the sixties and seventies. True to the music of his time, he was the melody rather than the rhythm. His voice was direct and served as a roadmap for millions. He detested confusion in thought or language.

The quality that impressed me the most about Mr. Fuller was the maturity and thoughtfulness of his responses. It seemed as though most of his answers were logical and consistent with his actions. He seldom spoke from the top of his head and was Black (culturally, consciously and in color), before it was popular, and always in an instructive and non-dogmatic manner. There was a hard morality to his presence without the self-righteousness. He represented that which was decent, human and right in this world. Mr. Fuller was a true lover of life and words. He traveled among many languages and cultures and was an emotionally voracious reader of international literature.

The pronoun "I" seldom cluttered his lexicon, and his sense of *style* was in the league of Duke Ellington and Gwendolyn Brooks. He took on the bullies of the world using carefully structured sentences that displayed educated urban metaphors, exemplifying a serious mind at work. He exhibited preparedness and winning possibilities. His dedication to young writers and creators helped to launch hundreds of poets, essayists, playwrights, novelists, visual artists, photographers and thinkers into the international arena. Hoyt Fuller was a "cultural" father to an entire generation of Black word-users. His uncompromising mind, his magic and music are missed. Few are able to sing his songs.

"compared to what," goes the song.
try example and originator.
try man of memory and legacy.
        man of destiny and future.
earthly visitor and runner among us,
suggesting *words* as mode and form,
        language morally precise,
demanding literacy and enlightenment,
as the ingredients for
beauty,
wisdom.

FIRST WORLD

(For Cheikh Anta Diop)

We were raised on the lower eastside of detroit,
close to harlem, new york, around the block from watts,
next to the mississippi delta in north america.
unaware of source or history, unaware of reasons,
whys or beginnings. accepting tarzan and she-woman,
accepting kong as king, accepting stanley-livingstone and
europecentric afrika, accepting british novels, french language
and portuguese folktales that devastated afrika's music &
magic, values and vision, people.

you helped restore memories,
gave us place and time,
positioned us within content and warnings,
centered us for the fire from the
first world:
original at dawn, founder of knowledge, inception. definer.
center of life, initial thinker, earliest, earliest order.
primary and wise, foremost, predominantly black, explainer,
mature pioneer, seer, roundrooted, earthlike, beginning tree,
cultivator, sourcegiver, genesis, entrance, tomorrow's light.
vision, unarguably afrikan.

278

REMARKABLE MUSIC AND MEASURE:
REMEMBERING THE FATHERS AND THE SONS
(For Chancellor Williams, Ossie Davis, Yosef ben Jochannan,
Hoyt W. Fuller, John H. Clarke and Hannibal Tirus Afrik)

these men
are alive & doing in this world.
all find the mediocre depressing and stimulating.

they function on sun & moon & mission.
their energy seldom dances within the
debilitating sight of others.
their expectations represent great challenge, clear motivation.

large moments exist between talkers and doers,
between original and carbon,
between infantile showboats and producers of brilliant
        tomorrows.

these men take the negative and create winning potentialities,
confronting fears
and discouraging the gossip of fools or foe,
discouraging smallness in all.

their women are remarkable music and measure,
bright desert dust, rugged fruit bearers,
expectors, of clear options and family-first,
anticipating men, answers, results.

magic of the dark spirit guides them
over the dirt of europe and votive of afrika,
equipping them to recognize the enemy, whether barbarians,
priests or cabinet members in the government of assassins.

they understand the failure we strap to our own dreams.
as others & most do the robot,
they compose new melodies and
choreograph the warrior's prayer.

---

rulers and leaders,
followers of demagogues and noise makers
with brains of floating rocks forever seek them out.

not born great,
they decided early not to swim in the
butt prints of others

selecting to conquer ignorance and evil,
selecting to run with ideas as others and many
knee-danced and drove mercedes over the rainbows of our
        children.

not born great,
they caused confusion in the tower,
worried captains of gun ships and
left large plants on this earth.

born like us, bronze and promising,
able to laugh and refuse greed in the wheat while
rejecting fairy tales and fashions from europe.

they are better, best and remarkable.
the measure of their music
is that certified fools and clowns
act intelligent in their light.

HONEST SEARCH

(For Bobby Wright)

with a mind as fast as a racetrack,
no wonder you were always running.

concerned about a people unaware of their own promise.

concerned about an answerless leadership lost
in material, status, pleasure acquisition

you did not dishonor the world, word or vision:
a fighter within the eye of the volcano,
a listener in the midst of the hurricane,
a lover unafraid of giving tears or laughter,
a scientist seeking bright and moving moments,
a deliverer of truths within the truths,
a tree rooted in history, beauty, permanence.
a good and honest man,
carrying wisdom.
carrying future.

we did not recognize greatness among us.

MOVES

(For Wilson Goode)

a negro playing mayor and hardball,
playing dirty harry and the buck stops here,
forgot where he came from with an eye on
where he is,

forgetting the children dark,
the women black,
the men afrikan,
whose hair, diet and ideas clashed with
where they and he are.

in the city of bells and love
for certain brothers,
a negro
plays white and mayor,
makes history in america
by disregarding the bill of rights
while dropping bombs on
who he used to be.

confirming and confirming
that america is still number one
in the manufacturing of
niggers.

282

POLLUTION: PART 1

a former jazz singer and
sideman to an imitation tap dance team,
recognizing his mediocrity
as a professional entertainer,
decided to use his gifts
in an area where competence is
uneven, less taxing and not measured
by melody or footmanship.

our singer-dancer
possessing the looks women adored,
having the rap men appreciated,
being the color negroes wished for,
endowed with the hair babies are born with,
insightful enough to peep the weaknesses
of his people,
changed his profession.

wilbert smith—
all 5' 11" of him—found a new name,
tailored his shirts,
bought a D.D. from a west coast jr. college,
picked up the
"most circulated book in the western world" and
      found god.

Poet: What Ever Happened to Luther?

he was strange weather, this luther. he read books, mainly
poetry and sometimes long books about people in foreign
places. for a young man he was too serious, he never did smile,
and the family still don't know if he had good teeth. he liked
music too, even tried to play the trumpet until he heard the
young miles davis. he then said that he'd try writing. the family
didn't believe him because there ain't never been no writers in
this family, and everybody knows that whatever you end up
doing, it's gotta be in your blood. it's like loving women, it's in
the blood, arteries and brains. this family don't even write let-
ters, they call everybody. thats why the phone is off 6 months
out of a year. then again, his brother willie t. use to write long,
long letters from prison about the books he was reading by
malcolm x, frantz fanon, george jackson, richard wright and oth-
ers. luther, unlike his brother, didn't smoke or drink and he'd
always be doing odd jobs to get money. even his closest friends
clyde and t. bone didn't fully understand him. while they be par-
tying all weekend, luther would be traveling. he would take his
little money with a bag full of food, mainly fruit, and a change of
underwear and get on the greyhound bus and go. he said he be
visiting cities. yet, the real funny thing about luther was his
ideas. he was always talking about afrika and black people. he
was into that black stuff and he was as light skinned as a piece
of golden corn on the cob. he'd be calling himself black and
afrikan and upsetting everybody, especially white people. they
be calling him crazy but not to his face. anyway the family,
mainly the educated side, just left him alone. they would just be
polite to him, and every child of god knows that when family
members act polite, that means that they don't want to be
around you. It didn't matter much because after his mother died
he left the city and went into the army. the last time we heard
from him was in 1963. he got put out the army for rioting. he
disappeared somewhere between mississippi and chicago. a
third cousin, who family was also polite to, appeared one day
and said that luther had grown a beard, changed his name and
stopped eating meat. she said that he had been to afrika and
now lived in chicago doing what he wanted to do, writing books,
she also said that he smiles a lot and kinda got good teeth.

THE GREAT WAIT

(it is possible that those persons who feel the need
to act against evil will be told to wait, be calm,
have patience, don't get upset, be realistic, don't rock
the boat, you are not so bad off, &c., &c.)

conscious tire of
waiting on waiters who wait for a living
as movers perfect the reasons why
others must wait.

movers say that waiting is an ancient art form
perfected by negroes waiting on something called *freedom*

that will surely come
if the waiters wait patiently in the kneeling position long
        enough.
long enough is when the waiter's knees shine and
head automatically drops whenever waiters are in the
        presence
of movers that tell them to be grateful
to have something to wait for.

movers say that afrikans can't even clothe themselves,
that the major occupation in central america is the
        maintenance of cemeteries,
that the people of asia need to control their sex drive,
that the only people that *really* understand modern
        technology are the south afrikaners and their brothers
        on pennsylvania avenue and
that the major problem for others is that they do not
        want to wait for their time.

most of the waiters are poor and miseducated.
waiting, like cocaine, is addictive.
people wait on welfare, workfare, healthfare, foodfare
and for businessmen and politicians to be fair.
waiters are line wise having spent a third of their lives
waiting in telephone lines, gas lines, light lines, bus lines,
        train lines and unemployment lines.

Killing Memory, Seeking Ancestors

waitin, waitin, tush, tush, tush.

waiters wait on presidents and first ladies to tell them
the secret of why waiting is better than
communism, socialism and hinduism,
why waiting is more uplifting than full employment
and is the coming tool to eliminate illiteracy and hunger.
waitin, waitin, tush.

western economists and sociologists have postulated that
waiting is the answer to family separations and ignorance.
that waiting will balance the budget and give waiters
the insight into why others care more about their condition
than they do.

the conscious world
waits on a people who have become
professional waiters.
the waiters' education clearly taught them
to aspire to become either the
waiter, waitee or waited.
for most wasted
waitin, waitin, tush, tush, tush.
popular consensus has it that
waiting builds character, cures dumbness and blindness,
waiting brings one closer to one's creator, waiting is intelligent
        work,
waiting is the fat person's answer to exercise
waiting will be featured on the johnny carson show this week
        disguised as
black urban professionals pushing the latest
form of waiting, "constructive engagement."
waitin, waitin, tush, tush, tush.
it is documented that
waiting will save the great whale population,
waiting will feed the children of the sudan,
waiting will stop acid rain,
waiting will save the great amazon rain forest,
waiting will guarantee disarmament and peace.

the major activity of waiters is watching television, sleeping,
eating junk foods and having frequent bowel movements.
waitin waitin tush tush tush tush

consciousness decays from
waitin on people with plastic bags
on their heads waitin
waitin on negroes that live for pleasure and money only waitin
waitin on a people that confuse freedom with handouts waitin
waitin on sam to straighten his spine and care for his children,
waiting on six child sue to say no,
waiting on $300 a day junkies,
waiting on a people whose heroes are mostly dead,
waitin on boldness from all this education we got,
waiting on the brother,
waiting on the sister.
waiting on waiters who wait for a living
as movers perfect the reasons why
others must wait.
waiting benefits non-waiters and their bankers.
most people are taught that
waiting is the misunderstood form of action,
is the act that is closest to sex and bar-b-q consumption.
waiting. waiting. waiting. waiting. waiting. waiting.
a truly universal art is practiced
by billions of people worldwide
who have been confirmed by their leaders
to be happy, satisfied and brain dead.

NEGRO: AN UPDATED DEFINITION PART 368

(for clarence pendleton and diana ross, to be read
to the popular song, "born in the USA")

negroes (negroes/knee grows) pc., -grows and devours itself;
invented around 1619 in the americas by the british, french,
spanish and portuguese. Also known as mulatto, creole, buck,
aborigine, quadroon, bitch, mixedblood, stud, half-breed,
uncle ben, aunt jemima, nigger and whatever.

BORN IN THE USA, THEY WAS BORN IN THE USA

negroes are treacherous and evil to own kind. major loyalty is
to anything, anybody lighter than black. hates the color of
coal, heats with gas or electricity, does not eat beans or fat-
back in public, hides from watermelon and neckbones. the
greens they eat is spinach, and they dress in the fashion of
calvin klein and anne klein II. males are mostly clean-shaved
but are known to wear mustaches. females shave legs and
are known to throw up at the sight of dirt under fingernails.

BORN IN THE USA, THEY WAS BORN

possessors of designer jeans, license plates and minds.
negroes have been bought and sold around the world with
minimum resistance. males and females are known to color
their faces and spend a good part of their days staring in mir-
rors and pressing their heads. it is not unusual for them to
have plastic surgery on their mouths, noses and feet. during
the early part of the century, the males' necks were used to
test the strength of ropes, and the females were considered,
except for pigs, the best breeders in the world.

BORN IN THE

288

negroes live beyond their means and enjoy socializing with people that don't like them. great gossipers and soap opera enthusiasts. many run or jog from the word *racism*. politics gives them headaches, and afrikan history is about as important as country music. most bow and say sir to anything wearing a tie and will die for country and general motors.

BORN

negroes live mainly in england, france, the carribean, united states, brazil and other places where europeans built churches, planted potatoes and put up barbed wire. The men die early and the women are alone most of the time, even when the men are alive. many are stockholders in mcdonalds and ibm and are lovers of cowboy and space movies.

THEY ARE BORN IN THE USA

negroes were reborn in such TV shows as *webster, gimme a break, the jeffersons, different strokes, benson, amen* and *miami vice*. they have currently captured the imagination of the world and hollywood in movies like *a soldier's story, the color purple* and *native son*. love money
more than self, love money more than self.
Negroes, the people that gave the world
billy dee williams and diahann carroll,
wake up and go to sleep praying,
"Thank God for Slavery."

THEY WERE MADE IN THE USA.

SEEKING ANCESTORS

(For the First Annual Egyptian Studies Conference, Los Angeles, California,
February 1984, organized by Maulana Karenga and Jacob Carruthers)

1.
what it was before deathtraps
before *thriller* and *beat it*, beat it
before soaps and reagan being raised to the station
of new redeemer by grandchildren viewing progress as
calvin klein & sonys in the ear.

where are the wise words,
the critical minds,
the questioners of sordid deeds,
the drinkers of pure water,
the doers of large moments?

what it was before emma lou planned her entire life
according to the stars & big sonny wilson hung on to every
syllable spoken by rev. ike, believe in me, and palm readers
from the pentagon?

what it is
is amnesia in america,
is memory the length of private parts,
is junk food masquerading as nutrition,
is projects and tenements replacing pyramids & space,
is fad posing as substance?

what it is
is strength measured by what you drink,
what you drive,
how you dress,
the texture of your hair
and the color of your woman,
"working hard for the money."

in america
working hard for the money
can get you bullets in the spine,
cocaine in the veins or a gold plated watch made in japan.
young death is guaranteed only if you think.
thinking in brazil & uganda,
in pakistan & south afrika is considered
contagious and dangerous.

shame and shock have evaporated.
grown men take their daughters and
boys hump boys and we are told that this
is modern, is normal, is in and
in america
where vacant heads copy & buy and
nourishment is derived from pepsis & cokes,
as vikings suck the blood of black people
draining the vision from the real miracles of the west
as we all approach the time when honor and integrity are
         obsolete
& preserved only in unread novels, unlistened music
as unattended grandmothers in michigan nursing homes
claim cats as family, friends and lovers.

291

2.
ever wonder where the circle came from
or who were the first people to use the triangle?
who were the original cultivators of the earth, who used
water of the nile to power minds and machines? what people
created music from instrument and voice and viewed the
building of cities as art and science? who were the
first to love because love contained the secrets of tomorrow?
look at yourselves.

there is magic in colors earthblack & purple issuing in
browns upon greens & oranges & others producing yellows
and ever present blue, skylike rain & water & warm.
today,
it is sure and dangerous to be dark in this universe.
there are secrets in color design,
there are mysteries in the making of the world,
there are complexities in the doings of strangers against the
            world.
there are clear courses that most minds are not ready for,
will never be able to perceive.
the west does serious damage to the mind.

america is not for sale, it is the buyer.

3.
we need clear language,
able storytellers,
discoverers of crops and seeds.
we need
decipherers and investigators of ideas & promise,
foreparents
screaming music that will arm us
with wisdom of the first,
warnings of
surrogate mothers and gene pool fathers.
we need
memory & moments, melody and song.
expanding vision
in search of winning ways and noble tomorrows.

comin back clearin eyes stompin, steppin, bolder
takin the wind & whispers seriously, takin the
slave beyond copy as cure, coping as necessity,
liftin the self & selves beyond rumor & wigs,
carrying the beauty of thought to completion,
knowing that if we think it,
doin it is only extension and reward
seekin to eclipse the expected to better & best.
if we have to beat it, beat it, try beatin the enemy,
try beatin those who reduced people to excretion & mannequins.

we were once music and might growin steel
we were beauty & find often feeling first drivin fire
we were seer & solution lift on up emma lou.
quiet step step
willinthefire, will in thefire, will in the fire
step step "dance to the music" step "dance to the music"
        step step
quiet and contemplative,
clearly conscious of wrongness
turn it around big sonny w. believe that
"we are family, my brothers, sisters & me."

4.
we conquered other selves in us
we became before we knew
tradition evaporated as others and many
stole the magic and wealth of millions.
diluting the dark people's walk & way,
cutting out the soul & source extricating the spirit
assassinating the common way.

Conquerors of vastness were
unable to copy lean steam
drumbeat walkers dancers carrying
spirit as gut & drive,
spirit as purpose and future
spirit as loving find,
as will & way
seeking beauty & meaning
in the secrets of ancient wall paintings
& buried souls.

5.
we are here
combat weary and willing
now & singing
looking special devoid of defeat
fired energy & hope imagining the inconceivable
here
urgently seeking lost records
igniting possibilities.

in the light of Amon and ancestors,
in the step of the clear and conscious,
it is beauty most needed in this place
as we recall that
by relinquishing building secrets

we lost clear water & children,
we lost future & wisdom & continuity.
we lost ourselves

demand
that the few & wise of us,
the monk & trane of us,
the careful & intelligent of us,
the hurston and dubois of us,
the silent and enduring of us,
the hansberry and woodson of us,
the conscious and loving of us,
to
recall the memory
to
recall the tradition & meaning
to rename the bringers
genius.
to quietly in the natural light of warm sunrises,
in the arms of loving smiles,
among the care of the consciously certain,
within the circle of the continued questioners,
to remember them ancestors all as

Killing Memory, Seeking Ancestors

dark & talented.
as
gifted light
bringers of source,
bringers of silence,
bringers of remembrance.

9

BLACK MEN

(1991)

THE B NETWORK

brothers bop & pop and be-bop in cities locked up
and chained insane by crack and other acts
of desperation computerized in pentagon cellars producing
boppin brothers boastin of being better, best & beautiful.

if the boppin brothers are beautiful where are the sisters
who seek brotherman with a drugless head unbossed or
        beaten
by the bodacious West?

in a time of big wind being blown by boastful brothers,
will other brothers beat back backwardness to better & best
without braggart bosses beatin butts,
takin names and diggin graves?

beatin badness into bad may be urban but is it beautiful &
        serious?
or is it betrayal in an era of prepared easy death hangin on
corners trappin young brothers before they know the
difference between big death and big life?

brothers bop & pop and be-bop in cities locked up
and chained insane by crack and other acts
of desperation computerized in pentagon cellars producing
boppin brothers boastin of being better, best, beautiful
and definitely not *Black*.

the critical best is that
brothers better be the best if they are to avoid backwardness
brothers better be the best if they are to conquer beautiful
        bigness
Comprehend that bad is only *bad* if it's big, Black and better
than boastful braggarts belittling our best and brightest
with bosses seeking inches when miles are better.

Black Men

brothers need to bop to being Black & bright & above board
the black train of beautiful wisdom that is bending this bind
toward a new & knowledgeable beginning that is
bountiful & bountiful & beautiful
While be-boppin to be
better than the test,
brotherman.

better yet write the exam.

BLACK MANHOOD: TOWARD A DEFINITION

your people first. a quiet strength. the positioning of oneself so that observation comes before reaction, where study is preferred to night life, where emotion is not seen as a weakness. love for self, family, children and extensions of self is beyond the verbal.

making your life accessible to children in meaningful ways. able to recognize the war we are in and doing anything to take care of family so long as it doesn't harm or negatively affect other Black people. willing to share resources to the maximum. willing to struggle unrelentingly against the evils of this world, especially evils that directly threaten the development of our people.

to seek and be that which is just, good and correct. properly positioning oneself in the context of our people. a listener, a student, a historian seeking hidden truths. one who develops leadership qualities and demands the same qualities of those who have been chosen to lead. sees material rewards as means toward an end and not an end in themselves. clean—mentally, spiritually and physically. protector of Black weak. one who respects elders. practical idealist, questioner of the universe and spiritually in tune with the best of the universe. honest and trusting, your word is your connector.

direction giver. husband. sensitive to Black women's needs and aspirations, realizing that it is not necessary for them to completely absorb themselves into us but that nothing separates the communication between us. a seeker of truth. a worker of the first order. teacher. example of what is to be. fighter. a builder with vision. connects land to liberation. a student of peace and war. statesman and warrior. one who is able to provide as well as receive. cullurally sound. creative. a motivator and stimulator of others.

a lover of life and all that is beautiful. one who is constantly growing and who learns from mistakes. a challenger of the known and the unknown. the first to admit that he does not know as he seeks to find out. able to solicit the best out of self and others. soft. strong. not afraid to take the lead. creative father. organized and organizer. a brother to brothers. a brother to sisters. understanding. parent. a winner. maintainer of the i can, i must, i will attitude toward Black struggle and life. a builder of the necessary. always and always in a process of growth and without a doubt believes that our values and traditions are not negotiable.

A BONDING

(For Susan and Khephra, August 20, 1989)

we were forest people.
landrooted. vegetable strong.
feet fastened to soil with earth strengthened toes.
determined fruit,
anchored
where music soared,
where dancers circled,
where writers sang,
where griots gave memory,
where smiles were not bought.

you have come to each other in wilderness,
in this time of cracked concrete, diminished vision, wounded
    rain.

at the center of flowers your craft is on fire.
only ask for what you can give.

do not forget bright mornings, hands touching under moon-
light, filtered water for your plants, healing laughter, renewing
futures. caring.

your search has been rewarded, marriage is not logical, it's
necessary. we have a way of running yellow lights, it is now
that we must claim
the sun in our hearts. your joining is a mending, a quilt.

as determined fruit
you have come late to this music,
only ask for what you can give.
you have asked for eachother.

MOTHERS

(for Mittie Travis (1897-1989), Maxine Graves Lee (1924-1959),
Inez Hall and GwendolynBrooks)

"Mothers are not to be confused with females
who only birth babies"

mountains have less height
and
elephants less weight than
mothers who plan bright futures for their children
against the sewers of western life.

mothers making magical music miles from monster madness
are not news,
are not subject for doctorates.

how shall we celebrate mothers?
how shall we call them in the winter of their lives?
what melody will cure slow bones?
who will bring them worriless late-years?
who will thank them for hidden pains?

mothers are not broken-homes,
they are irreplaceable fire,
a kiss or smile at a critical juncture,
a hug or reprimand when doubts swim in,
a calm glance when the world seems impossible,
the back that america could not break.

mothers making magical music miles from monster madness
are not news,
are not subject for doctorates.

mothers instill questions and common sense,
urge mighty thoughts and lively expectations,
are impetus for discipline and intelligent work while
making childhood exciting, unforgettable and challenging.

mothers are preventative medicine
they are
women who hold their children all night to break fevers,
women who cleaned other folks' homes in order to give their
children one,
women who listen when others laugh,
women who believe in their children's dreams,
women who lick the bruises of their children and
give up their food as they suffer hunger pains silently.

if mothers depart their precious spaces too early
values, traditions and bonding interiors are wounded,
morals confused, ethics unknown, needed examples absent
and
crippling histories of other people's victories are passed on as
knowledge.

mothers are not broken-homes,
they are gifts
sharing full hearts, friendships and mysteries.
as the legs of fathers are amputated
mothers double their giving
having seen the deadly future of white flowers.

mothers making magical music miles from monster madness
are not news,
are not subject for doctorates.

who will bring them juice in the sunset of their time?
who will celebrate the wisdom of their lives,
the centrality of their songs,
the quietness of their love,
the greatness of their dance?
it must be us,
able daughters, good sons
their cultural gift,
the fruits and vegetables of their medicine.

We must come like earthrich waterfalls.

YES

for those that want:
every woman a man
every man a woman,
every person an education and willing work,
for all people
family, food, clothing, shelter, love,
frequent smiles and children swimming in glorious happiness.

for every elder a home, blooming health, few worries,
good teeth and fun-filled thank yous.
for all people,
liberating culture,
the full love of laughing children who
have been bathed in the caring eyes of
family, friends, nation.

for all people,
the inner glow that radiates peace and wisdom,
the confirming smiles of knowledge known,
the confident walk of music heard,
the quiet presence of having accepted and created beauty.

for Afrikan people
an unspoken understanding that
this is the center we gave the world

this is civilization.

10
CLAIMING EARTH
(1994)

CULTURE

The culture of a people is their definition.

The African/Black in us is the water, earth, air, fire and wind forming the core that produces the fuel energizing the spirits and souls that center our creation.

The sum total of a peoples' existence is exhibited in their culture, from the food grown, prepared and consumed to the clothes they make and wear, the god(s) they worship and the spirit manifested as a result of that worship, the music calling the drum in them producing the dance that glues them together in sharing movement and oneness, the visual art that replicates their souls and ideas for the others and themselves to see, the words—oral and written—marking their existence that form the history and heritage of each moment catching all new creations in fiction and non-fiction, poetry disguised as song and drama in melodies that move the feet of the bodies toward the transportation that carries them throughout the planet especially among their own villages, towns and cities that ultimately harnesses the depth, the beauty, the ugliness, the technically unusable, the happiness, the magnificence, the rottenness, the kindness, the love, the rough-rawness, the refined carefulness, the unusual thoughtfulness, the occasional queerness, the quiet unexpectedness, an economy of fairness, the ripe laughter, the largeness and smallness of our souls, to the war and peace in each of us: confirming culture.

The culture of a people represents life, source, soul, spirit, saneness, silliness, science, smiles, seriousness and connectedness: family.

This familyhood confirms and confirms
in an undying love that is burned into the souls of each
newborn
binding them biologically and culturally
to life, source, spirit saneness, smiles, seriousness and
memory that
passes on immortality,

passes on the heartbeats of genius,
passes on respect for others,
passes on earthgrown love,
passes on the permanence of family,
community, nation, people, culminating in the unique
celebration of themselves.
spirited community.

This is culture. replicate.

HAITI

(for the Haitian people and Randall Robinson)

in haiti at wahoo bay beach of port-au-prince
there are beautiful women in bathing suits
with men who are young, light-skinned and rich.
you are welcomed if you run with the right wolves.

in port-au-prince, on the other side of the water
fenced off from wahoo bay beach
a few children receive 19th century education in
one room shanties without running water or toilets.
their parents cook on outdoor woodfires and
pass waste in secret spots or community latrines.
they live in poverty within poverty and they elected a   priest
to represent their dreams.
he promised food, clean water, education, wood, seeds,
        fairness, democracy and peace on earth.

the people of haiti are angry with u.s. presidents.
the haitian military forced their elected priest to flee in the
night, with their dreams and prayers
in a quickly packed suitcase.

the people are uneducated, not stupid.
democracy is coming to south africa and
haiti drowns in white promises.
bill clinton talks in codes as
paramilitary terror squads beat patriotism into the people.
american businesses pay 14 cents an hour to the peasants
and
provide japanese toys and airline tickets to the elite.

the people of haiti are angry with u.s. presidents.
they take boat rides by the thousands
to cross a sea made of their dead for america.
most are returned on military ships,
unsuitable as political refugees.
we are told that *race* is not the problem
it is the island, its not cuba.

the rich in haiti diet,
the poor starve and disappear if they complain too loudly.
randall robinson lived on water and tomato juice
his eyes sank into his forehead for a month.
his eyes are clear and so is he.

the new duvalierists rule a dirty capital,
when rain comes the people join the mud,
the rich drive jeeps made in the U.S.
the "MREs"—morally repugnant elite—are like elite
everywhere:
they do not feel for others,
they hide their eyes,
they wear foreign made clothes,
their children have private playgrounds and educations,
they live on hills and laugh at the dark people who don 't
even own the night.
they speak the language of killers.

WHITE PEOPLE ARE PEOPLE TOO

(For Mead, Hillman, Bly, Densmore, and Multicultural Men's Work)

Most struggles have a way of homogenizing people,
of devaluing individuality
always looking at the big suffering revolutionary picture,
our pains inhibit seeing beyond our struggle,
beyond culture, beyond race.

race struggle can be cleansing and uplifting,
race struggle can be blinding and self-righteous,
race struggle seldom separates the evil from the ignorant,
    "bad and not so bad, good and not so good, best and better,"
race struggle minimizes intrarace struggle.

parts of a lifetime are lost documenting the enemy.
in struggle
we only know each other and
each other is not the world

it is not in me to love an enemy
who has committed horrific crimes against children.
are crimes transferrable?
are crimes inherited by sons and daughters
who reject that history
and work for reconciliation and reparations?
can being Black and African-centered guide me to the
centering best of Asians, Europeans, Native Americans,
indigenous peoples, women, others?

it is in me to grow.
to walk among vegetation and cultures, to think.
it is in me to see that pain is colorless
it is in me to value the differences of others.

It is human to share,
I am not suicidal.

313

Claiming Earth

Rwanda:
Where Tears have no Power

Who has the moral high ground?

Fifteen blocks from the whitehouse
on small corners in northwest, d.c.
boys disguised as men rip each other's hearts out
with weapons made in china. they fight for territory.

across the planet in a land where civilization was born
the boys of d.c. know nothing about their distant relatives
in rwanda. they have never heard of the hutu or tutsi people.
their eyes draw blanks at the mention of kigali, byumba
or butare. all they know are the streets of d.c., and do not
cry at funerals anymore. numbers and frequency have a way
of making murder commonplace and not news
unless it spreads outside of our house, block, territory.

modern massacres are intraethnic. bosnia, sri lanka, burundi,
nagorno-karabakh, iraq, laos, angola, liberia and rwanda are
small foreign names on a map made in europe. when bodies
by the tens of thousands float down a river turning the water
the color of blood, as a quarter of a million people flee bare-
foot into tanzania, somehow we notice. we do not smile, we
have no more tears. we hold our thoughts in a deeply muted
silence looking south and thinking that today
nelson mandela seems much larger
than he is.

GWENDOLYN BROOKS:
DISTINCTIVE AND PROUD AT 77

how do we greet significant people among us,
what is the area code that glues them to us,
who lights the sun burning in their hearts,
where stands their truths in these days of MTV
    and ethnic cleansing,
what language is the language of Blacks?

she has a map in her. she always returns home. we are not
open prairie, we are rural concrete written out of history. she
reminds us of what we can become, not political correctness
or social commentators and not excuse makers for Big peo-
ple. always a credit-giver for ideas originated in the quiet of
her many contemplations. a big thinker is she. sleeps with
paper and dictionary by her bed, sleeps with children in her
head. her first and second drafts are pen on paper. her hus-
band thinks he underestimates her. she thinks we all have
possibilities. nothing is simplified or simply given. she wears
her love in her language. if you do not listen, you will miss her
secrets. we do not occupy the margins of her heart, we are
the blood, soul, Black richness, spirit and water-source pump-
ing the music she speaks. uncluttered by people worship, she
lives always on the edge of significant discovery. her instruc-
tion is "rise to the occasion," her religion is "kindness," her
work is sharing and making words matter. she gives to the
people everybody takes from.
she is grounded-seeker. cultured-boned.
she is Black sunset and at 77 is no amateur.
rooted willingly and firmly in dark soil, she is last of the great
oaks.
name her poet.
as it does us, her language needs to blanket the earth.

315

11
GROUNDWORK
(1996)

STANDING AS AN AFRICAN MAN:
BLACK MEN IN A SEA OF WHITENESS

Where do I belong and what is the price I have to pay for being where and who I am?

Study the faces of children who look like you. Walk your streets. Count the smiles and bright eyes, and make a mental note of their ages. At what age do our children cease to smile naturally, smile full-teeth, uninhibited, expecting full life? At what age will memory of lost friends, and lost relatives, deaden their eyes? Where does childhood stop in much of our community? At seven, eight? How many killings, rapes, beatings, verbal and mental abuse, hustles, get-over programs, drug infestations, drive-by shootings/drive-by leaders must they witness before their eyes dry up for good and their only thought is, "Will I make it to the age of twenty-five?" When the life in the eyes of our children does not gleam brightly with future and hope, we cease being nurturers and become repairers of broken spirits and stolen souls. This is the state we are now in and too often it is too late.

Where do I belong and what is the price I have to pay for being where and who I am?

If you don't know, you can't do.

From whom do we buy our food? From whom do we rent our apartments? From whom do we buy our clothes, furniture, cars, and life-bettering needs? On whose land do we walk, sleep, live, play, work, get high, chase women, lie, steal, produce children, and die? Why is it that 800,000 Black men and 50,000 Black women populate the nation's prisons? Is race a factor in a land where white people control most things of value? Is race a factor in a country where young Black boys and men are dying quicker than their birth rate? When do we declare war on our own destruction? Why is it that the Blacker one is the worse it is? Who taught Black people that killing Black people is alright and sometimes honorable?

This is Our Charge!

Study the landscape. Read the music in your hearts. Remember the beauty of mothers, sisters, and the women in our lives who talked good about us. Remember when we talked good about us. Remember when we talked good about them. Understand the importance of ideas.

This is Our Mission!

Pick up a book. Challenge the you in you. Rise above the limited expectations of people who do not like you and never will like you. Rise above the self-hatred that slowly eats your heart, mind, and spirit away. Find like-minded brothers. Study together. Talk together. Find each others' hearts. Ask the right questions. Why are we poor? Why are our children not educated? Why are our children dying at such an unbelievable rate? Why are we landless? What does land ownership have to do with race? What does wealth have to do with race? Why do we hate being called African and Black? What does Africa mean to me, us? Why is Africa in a state of confusion and civil war? Why is there no work in our communities? What is the difference between a producer and a consumer? What do we produce that is sold and used worldwide? Whose knowledge is most valuable for the development of Black (African) people? Would I kill myself and others who look like me if I loved myself and those who look like me? From where does self-love come? Who taught me, us, self-hatred? Is self-hatred an idea? Is self-love an idea? To whose ideas do we tapdance? With whose ideas do we impress each other? Are African (Black) ideas crucial to our discourse and development? Can a Black person be multicultural if he/she does not have his/her culture first? When do we declare war on ignorance, intellectual betrayal, self-destruction, pimpism, weakening pleasures, European worldviews, beggar mentalities, and white world supremacy? Is race an idea? When will we use the race idea to benefit us?

Where do I belong and what is the price I have to pay for being where and who I am?
We belong among the people worldwide who look like us. We belong to a world where we produce rather than consume. We belong to a world where the measurement of Black beauty and worth is internal and cultural.

We belong where our education is not anti-us.
We belong among African men who are brothers and brothers who are Africans. How will we recognize them?

You will recognize your brothers
by the way they act and move throughout the world.
there will be a strange force about them,
there will be unspoken answers in them.
this will be obvious not only to you but to many.
the confidence they have in themselves and in
their people will be evident in their quiet saneness.
the way they relate to women will be
clean, complimentary, responsible, with honesty and as
  partners.
the way they relate to children will be
strong and soft full of positive direction and as example.
the way they relate to men
will be that of questioning our position in this world,
will be one of planning for movement and change,
will be one of working for their people,
will be one of gaining and maintaining trust within the
  culture.
these men at first will seem strange and unusual but
this will not be the case for long.
they will train others and the discipline they display
will be a way of life for many.
they know that this is difficult
but this is the life that they have chosen
for themselves, for us, for life:
they will be the examples,
they will be the answers, they will be the first-line builders,
they will be the creators,
they will be the first to give up the weakening pleasures,
they will be the first to share a black value system,
they will be the workers,
they will be the scholars,
they will be the providers,
they will be the historians,
they will be the doctors, lawyers, farmers, priests
and all that is needed for development and growth.
you will recognize these brothers
and
they will not betray you.

THE MISSION OF A GOOD MAN

(For Robert J. Dale at fifty)

we must read this man differently
dark-skinned children are at the center of his heart.

he possesses a desperate joy,
few pleasures, easy laughter,
he takes time to hear
little voices.

his thoughts are reclusive, private, complex.
he lives among a community
that understands & calls his name often and
thinks that he is a mountain,
thinks that he is rice milk & precious stone.
they see him the way he sees our children. honestly.

his interior is tree lined, African wheat grass, mountainous.
he has a suffering smile that understands voluminous truths.
he must make a payroll twice monthly,
        make deals with pants-wearing roaches with
        deep immune systems & bent smiles requiring him
        to bathe & meditate frequently. he says,
        for our children we must claim part of the map,
        geography is not european, is not white, must not
        be foreign to us.

we must receive this man accurately, traditionally.
dark-skinned children are at the heart of his center.

his heart is African.

THE STATE'S ANSWER TO ECONOMIC DEVOLOPMENT

it is the poor
that populate Las Vegas & riverboat casinos
where neon lights & one-armed bandits never die
yet draw the young
and aged whose lives
seem exhausted & bored beside
the lights,
the games,
the entertainment,
the unchances,
the early hope
where everybody can afford
a hotel room to drop a suitcase
with fresh greyhound tags notating
the midnight ride from California & elsewhere
with $300 in their left shoes
that they think
will win them a life.

323

So Many Books, So Little Time

(For librarians & independent booksellers)

Frequently during my mornings of pain & reflection
when I can't write
or articulate my thoughts
or locate the mindmusic needed
to complete the poems & essays
that are weeks plus days overdue
forcing me to stop, I say cease
answering my phone, eating right, running my miles,
reading my mail and making love.
(Also, this is when my children do not seek me out
because I do not seek them out)
I escape north to the nearest library or used bookstore.
They are my retreats, my quiet energy/givers, my intellectual
        refuge.

For me it is not bluewater beaches, theme parks
or silent chapels hidden among forest greens.
Not multistored American malls, corporate book
supermarkets, mountain trails or Caribbean hideaways

My sanctuaries are liberated lighthouses of shelved books,
featuring forgotten poets, unread anthropologists &
playwrights; starring careful anthologists of art & photography,
upstart literary critics; introducing dissertations of tenure-
seeking assistant professors, self-published geniuses, remain-
dered first novelists; highlighting speed-written bestsellers,
wise historians & theologians, nobel & pulitzer prize winning
poets & fiction writers, overcertain political commentators,
small press wonderkinds & learned academics.
All are vitamins for my slow brain & sidetracked spirit in this
winter of creating.

I do not believe in smiling politicians, AMA doctors,
zebra-faced bankers, red-jacketed real estate or automobile
salespoeple or singing preachers.

I believe in books,
it can be conveniently argued that knowledge,
not that which is condensed or computer packaged, but
pages of hard-fought words, dancing language
meticulously & contemplatively written by the likes of
   me & others,
shelved imperfectly at the levels of open hearts & minds
is preventive medicine strengthening me for the return to my
clear pages of incomplete ideas to be reworked, revised &
written as new worlds and words in all of their subjective con-
figurations to eventually be processed into books that will
hopefully be placed on the shelves of libraries &
bookstores to be found & browsed over by receptive
booklovers, readers & writers looking for a retreat,
looking for departure & home,
looking for open heart surgery without the knife.

Too Many of Our Young are Dying

moments represent a lifetime.

our hearts lose sunshine
when our children cease to smile words
and share with parents their passionate pain.
our children, in the millions
are dropping from the trees of life too soon,
their innocent hearts and bodies
are forced to navigate within modern madness,
searching for life and love
in the basements of a crippled metropolis,
a disintegrating culture   too soon.

are we not all earth & lakes & sun?
are we not all mamas & babas to their young music?
their lives are not abstracted bragging rights,
we must never stop listening to their stories & songs.

when our children
do not share their young pain
it is a sign of our closed ears and punctured hearts
do not misread the silences in their eyes,
they are seeking sunshine from us
immediately.

WHAT MAKES HIM HAPPY

this woman who loves black & white photographs is
brightfaced, blessed with deep-rooted & perspicuous eyes,
carries one hundred & thirty-five pounds of tall,
lean beauty draped on African bones uses
liquid soap that smells of peppermint or almond;
drives her car barefooted.

she appreciates the difficult differences
between Toni Morrison and William Faulkner,
understands that the free market is really a family affair,
has tasted and lost profound love and experienced
the pain and miracle of giving birth.
this woman runs a mile in under nine minutes
and believes that billie holiday, john coltrane &
louis armstrong are alive & still swingin, says
she loves vegetables, brown rice, nectarines & her son.

she relaxes with films that need subtitles,
music that requires a mind and her man
who is comfortable with complexity and enchantment.
she is contemplative about romare bearden's signature on his
        paintings,
& has a smile that evokes volcanoes in men.
she has god in her heart but doesn't brag about it,
prefers baths to showers & sweetens her body with
        olive/aloe oil.
her home is art-full as are the five rings decorating her fingers
        & ears,
her hair is shaped close to her head which she cuts herself,
she has a museum of a memory & articulates her love and
thoughts firmly and passionately while listening to
billie, trane & pops collaborating
in black & blue eight-scale harmonies
the music, the traditions & the *way* of our tomorrows.

A Calling

(for Rev. Frank Madison Reid III
on the occasion of 25 years of service in the ministry)

we are short memory people,
too willing to settle for artless resumes of
rapid life   brief prayers   cappuccino.

our young adapt to contemporary clothing without question,
as we fail to acknowledge brilliance among us
displaying a hesitancy to tell this preacherman, this good
          brother
how his journey has become our journey.
in him is ordered-calm, deep thought, quality-love, a probing
          mind.

are pastors inspired to read Baldwin, Morrison, Diop,
Chomsky, Said and Brooks? are their ears prepared for
Monk, Aretha, Trane, Chuck D and music screaming for the
tongues of hypocrites? can a serious minister be known for
anything other than knowing God's name, being clean, loving
his family and saying double yes to fried chicken dinners?
cultural essentiality?

we are short memory people,
you have been planted among us
artfully seeded in Black earth to illuminate the texts,
shepherd our prayers, spiritualize our commitments and
help us seal the holes in our souls.

some arrogantly shout that this is your job,
in kind smiles and rather meditatively, others voice
we don't remember you ever filling out an
          employment application.

About the Author

As poet, publisher, editor, and educator, Haki R. Madhubuti serves as a pivotal figure in the development of a strong Black literary tradition. He has published 19 books and is a much soughtafter poet and lecturer in the U.S. and abroad. In 1991 he received the American Book Award and was named Author of the Year for the State of Illinois by the Illinois Association of Teachers of English.

Madhubuti was the recipient of the National Endowment for the Arts, National Endowment for the Humanities fellowships and Ilinois Arts Council Award. In 1993 he received the Paul Robeson Award from the African-American Arts Alliance and the Lifetime Visionary Award from the African Poetry Theater, Inc. Mr. Madhubuti was instrumental in establishing the historic May 6, 1995 meeting between Dr. Betty Shabazz (widow of Malcolm X) and Minister Louis Farrakhan of the Nation of Islam. He also served on the organizing body of the African American Leadership Summit and was a member of the Executive Council and speaker at the historic Million Man March, October 16, 1995.

A proponent of independent Black institutions, Mr. Madhubuti is the founder of Third World Press, Black Books Bulletin, African-American Book Center (1974-1995), and co-founder of the Institute of Positive Education/New Concept Development Center. He is also a founder and board member of the National Association of Black Book Publishers. He has been poet-in-residence at Cornell University, University of Illinois at Chicago, Howard University, and Central State University.

Haki Madhubuti earned his MFA from the University of Iowa and was awarded the Doctor of Humane Letters from DePaul University and Sojourner-Douglass College in June, 1996. He is currently a professor of English and Director of the Gwendolyn Brooks Center at Chicago State University. He lives in Chicago with his wife, Dr. Safisha Madhubuti, and their children, Laini, Bomani, and Akili.